OXBOW INSIGHTS IN

MYTH AND MATERIALITY

John Waddell

OXBOW | books
Oxford & Philadelphia

Published in the United Kingdom in 2018 by
OXBOW BOOKS
The Old Music Hall, 106–108 Cowley Road, Oxford OX4 1JE

and in the United States by
OXBOW BOOKS
1950 Lawrence Road, Havertown, PA 19083

© John Waddell 2018

Paperback Edition: ISBN 978-1-78570-975-3
Digital Edition: ISBN 978-1-78570-976-0 (epub)

A CIP record for this book is available from the British Library

Library of Congress Control Number: 2018935377

All rights reserved. No part of this book may be reproduced or transmitted in any form or by any means, electronic or mechanical including photocopying, recording or by any information storage and retrieval system, without permission from the publisher in writing.

For a complete list of Oxbow titles, please contact:

United Kingdom	United States of America
Oxbow Books	Oxbow Books
Telephone (01865) 241249	Telephone (800) 791-9354
Fax (01865) 794449	Fax (610) 853-9146
Email: oxbow@oxbowbooks.com	Email: queries@casemateacademic.com
www.oxbowbooks.com	www.casemateacademic.com/oxbow

Oxbow Books is part of the Casemate group

Front cover: Cú Chulainn and the Morrígan in the form of a raven on a cattle raid. From T. W. Rolleston, *Myths & Legends of the Celtic Race*, 1911; illustration by J. C. Leyendecker.
Back cover: *(top to bottom)*: The 'Banqueting Hall' on the Hill of Tara; stone statue found at the Glauberg; the Leubingen tumulus.

Printed and bound in Great Britain by Marston Book Services Ltd, Oxfordshire

... in the course of human events societies pass and religious systems change; the historical landscape is littered with the husks of desiccated myths. These are valuable nonmaterial fossils of mankind's recorded history, especially if still embedded in layers of embalmed religion, as part of a stratum of tradition complete with cult, liturgy and ritual. Yet equally important is the next level of transmission, in which the sacred narrative has already been secularized, myth has been turned into saga, sacred time into heroic past, gods into heroes and mythical action into 'historical plot'.

Jaan Puhvel, *Comparative Mythology* (1987)

OXBOW INSIGHTS IN ARCHAEOLOGY

EDITORIAL BOARD

Richard Bradley – Chair
Umberto Albarella
Michael J. Allen
John Baines
Ofer Bar-Yosef
Chris Gosden

Simon James
Neil Price
Anthony Snodgrass
Rick Schulting
Mark White
Alasdair Whittle

Contents

Acknowledgements vii
List of Illustrations ix

Introduction 1
1. The Invented Past 10
2. The Mythic Past 29
3. Sacral Kingship – The Mythology 37
4. Kings in Archaeology 56
5. The Otherworld 80
6. The Sacred Tree 106
7. The Ancestors of Epona 124
Epilogue 147

Notes 152
References 162

Acknowledgements

I am very grateful to all who have helped with the production of this work especially Conor Newman and Jane Conroy. I am also particularly grateful to Richard Bradley for his encouragement. Dr Elizabeth O'Brien kindly provided some additional information on the Farta burial. Máirín Ní Dhonnchadha was, as ever, a source of sound advice. 'The Connacht Project' in the National University of Ireland Galway – under her direction – was an important stimulus. This is an interdisciplinary research initiative that investigates aspects of the exceptionally rich corpus of early Irish texts relating to the ancient province of Connacht. Its archaeological component addresses the challenges posed by a number of western sites and monuments, like the royal complex of Rathcroghan, where myth, history and archaeology converge. Both Jane Conroy and Angela Gallagher deserve special thanks for their assistance with the illustrations.

The sources of the illustrations are as follows: 1.1. Author. 1.2. J. Cooke in his 1903 edition of W. F. Wakeman's *Hand-book of Irish Antiquities*; The image of 'The bier of King Dathi carried in the Alps' comes from John Boyle O'Reilly's *Irish Songs and Ballads* (1888). 1.3. Courtesy of Conor Newman. 1.4. Macalister 1919. 1.5. Lynn 1997 (© Crown DfC); Mallory 1985. 1.6. Lynn 2002. 3.1. Courtesy of the Discovery Programme.

4.1. Eogan 2001; Fritsch 2010. 4.2. Raftery 1983; Armstrong 1933. 4.3. Parfitt 1995. 4.4. Hansen 2010. 4.5 Fritsch 2010. 4.6. After Lawson 2007. 4.7. After Scarre 2013 with emendations. 5.1. Harrison 2004. 5.2. After Stead 1991. 5.3. Shepherd and Shepherd 2001; Cahill and Sikora 2011. 5.4. Jones 1984; Ellis 1942. 5.5. Raftery 1983; Ó Floinn 2009. 5.6. 1–3: Jope 2000; 4: Stead and Hughes 1997. 5.7. 1–2: Kaul 1998; 3: Aner and Kersten 1976. 5.8. Kristiansen 2010. 5.9. 1: Patay 1990; 2–3: Wirth 2006; 4: Rolley 2003.

6.1. After Wyss 1954; Brennand and Taylor 2003. 6.2. Andrén 2014. 6.3. Tonnochy and Hawkes 1931; Marco-Simón 1998. 6.4. A: Lynn 1997 (© Crown DfC); B: Mallory 1985; C: Auboyer 1959. 6.5. Powell 1971. 6.6. 1, 4: Stollner 2014; 3: Ginoux 2007; 4: Jacobsthal 1944. 7.1. Koch 2010. 7.2. 1–4: Duval 1987, 5: Duval 1975. 7.3. Giraud 2015. 7.4. Méniel 1992. 7.5. Stead 1991. 7.6. Collins 1952. Back cover photo: the Leubingen tumulus: author 2009.

List of Illustrations

Fig. 1.1. Rathcroghan Mound and the results of geophysical survey.
Fig. 1.2. Dathi's Mound at Rathcroghan and 'The bier of King Dathi carried in the Alps'.
Fig. 1.3. The 'Banqueting Hall' on the Hill of Tara.
Fig. 1.4. Medieval drawing of the great Banqueting Hall on the Hill of Tara and R. A. S. Macalister's reconstruction.
Fig. 1.5. Plan of Navan Fort and an artist's impression of Navan Fort today.
Fig. 1.6. Schematic plan of Navan Site A–C and the sequence of circular enclosures at Site B.
Fig. 3.1. LiDAR image of the Hill of Tara.
Fig. 4.1. Bronze cardiophylax from Loughnaneane, Co. Roscommon, and a stone statue from Capestrano.
Fig. 4.2. Gold torcs from Knock and gold beads from Tumna, Co. Roscommon.
Fig. 4.3. Burial at Mill Hill, Deal, Kent.
Fig. 4.4. Reconstruction of the Hochdorf burial.
Fig. 4.5. Stone statue found at the Glauberg.
Fig. 4.6. Reconstructed plan of the Bush Barrow burial dug in 1808.
Fig. 4.7. A pattern of social stratification in prehistoric Europe.
Fig. 5.1. Engraved slab from Cabeza de Buey, Badajoz.
Fig. 5.2. Chariot grave at Kirkburn, Yorkshire.
Fig. 5.3. Inverted pottery from Findhorn, Moray, and Ballyvool, Co. Kilkenny.
Fig. 5.4. Scenes from Nordic mythology: picture-stone at Tängelgårda, Gotland, and a wooden carving from Hylestad, Norway.
Fig. 5.5. Solar imagery: the Petrie Crown and pairs of bronze discs.
Fig. 5.6. Solar imagery: the Battersea shield, the Aylesford bucket and two mirrors.

Fig. 5.7. Solar journeys: bronze razors and the Trundholm 'chariot of the sun'.
Fig. 5.8. Upright and inverted boats in Scandinavian rock art.
Fig. 5.9. Solar images on bronzes.
Fig. 6.1. Sacred trees 2000 years apart.
Fig. 6.2. Scandinavian tree settings.
Fig. 6.3. Image of sacred trees from Rivenhall, Essex, and Arcóbriga, Spain.
Fig. 6.4. The *axis mundi* and the solar wheel at Navan and Amaravati.
Fig. 6.5. Sketch of a panel on the Gundestrup cauldron.
Fig. 6.6. Stylized sacred trees on belt-hooks and a scabbard.
Fig. 7.1. The Ekurini inscription.
Fig. 7.2. Coins of the Redones.
Fig. 7.3. A horse burial found at Cagny (Normandy).
Fig. 7.4. Sacrificed stallions at Vertault (Côte d'Or).
Fig. 7.5. Horse burial found at Kirkburn, Yorkshire.
Fig. 7.6. Plan of the hillfort at Blewburton Hill, Oxfordshire.

Introduction

Famous places like Tara, Co. Meath, and Navan, Co. Armagh, are called 'royal sites' because they are closely associated with kings and queens in medieval myth and legend. Surprisingly, perhaps, they also have Otherworldly links for supernatural beings are frequent visitors, and these are sometimes friendly, sometimes hostile. For the poet W. B. Yeats, however, this Otherworld was a place where 'where beauty has no ebb, decay no flood, but joy is wisdom, time an endless song'. I know of one gateway to this magical realm and I was first able to stand on its threshold many years ago when investigating the archaeology of Rathcroghan, a royal site in the west of Ireland. Like Tara, this is a complex of ancient monuments that figures prominently in Irish medieval literature and carries an outstanding weight of myth and legend.

Unlike Tara, it has an entrance to this Otherworld, the *síd* or otherworldly place of ancient Crúachain as it is called in early Irish, and we shall explore it in due course. The early study of Rathcroghan's monuments did confirm its archaeological importance, a conclusion strengthened by extensive geophysical survey there in the 1990s, but I was at a loss to explain why medieval story tellers should leave us a picture of a prehistoric royal settlement with such puzzling otherworldly associations. Indeed I ended my paper with the question how does an archaeologist recapture the importance of an entrance to an Otherworld?[1] Part of the answer lies in its mythology.

The aim of this book is to promote the thesis that myth may illuminate archaeology and that on occasion archaeology may shed light on myth using Irish evidence as a starting point. Medieval Irish literature is rich in mythic themes that in some cases at least may prompt archaeologists to take a fresh look at the materials they investigate. Some of these themes are of great antiquity but some elements were invented by contemporary authors in the middle ages. It is a challenging source as I indicated in an earlier study, *Archaeology and Celtic Myth*, published in 2014. It is not always easy to distinguish a genuine archaism from a medieval invention – and, to complicate the picture, there is plenty of evidence of Classical and Christian influences in this material too.

Early Irish literature is written in Old Irish (roughly AD 600–900) and Middle Irish (approximately AD 900–1200). It is the richest literary legacy in a Celtic language and is unique in both volume and range. It is by far the largest body of written material in a non-Latin tongue in western Europe. The narrative literature includes the Ulster or Heroic Cycle of tales where Rathcroghan figures prominently as the splendid court of Queen Medb and her husband Ailill, king of Connacht. Her royal residence was the rath or fort of Crúachain – a great mound in the centre of the Rathcroghan complex. That extensive geophysical survey just mentioned demonstrated that this mound was a ceremonial monument with a protracted prehistory and not a habitation site. There is clearly a significant divergence between text and archaeology. Yet it is the mythology attached to Rathcroghan that gives us some idea of the role this site may have had and the rituals that may have been practised there in pre-Christian times. The same may be said about the other major royal sites: Navan Fort – the Emain Macha of these medieval tales – and Tara.

Among the numerous mythic themes in these medieval texts, some are certainly of archaeological interest because they may reveal something about the prehistoric past not just in Ireland but elsewhere in Europe too. Each of these royal sites had their associated goddess of sovereignty who played a key role in the inauguration rites of successive kings. Representing the land and fertility, these divinities had martial and equine aspects as well. Besides a belief in a complex Otherworld and these sovereignty figures, allusions to the institution of sacral kingship recur again and again. The medieval evidence leaves no doubt that sacral kingship was a prehistoric tradition in ancient

Ireland. Its decline in early Christian times was hastened by the rise of a multitude of medieval kin groups. This process culminated in great dynasties such as the Uí Néill in the east and north, the Uí Bhriain in Munster and the Uí Chonchobair in Connacht whose modern namesakes, O'Neills, O'Briens and O'Conors, are now scattered around the world.

Female deities, sacral kings and the Otherworld are just some of the major themes that may have left traces in the archaeological record. Their origins may lie in an Indo-European world and take us back to the Bronze Age – if not before in some cases. Most European languages belong to the Indo-European language family and with few exceptions (such as Basque and Finnish) today's linguistic landscape has been fashioned by this inheritance. Further afield, the Hittite language is recorded in cuneiform script on clay tablets in Anatolia around 1700 BC. The oldest texts, in Indo-Iranian, are in Vedic Sanskrit and appear in the 2nd millennium BC as does Mycenaean Greek. In Europe, Celtic and Italic languages are attested in the 1st millennium BC. No scholar of Irish, Welsh or Continental Celtic will deny the Indo-European origins of these languages. Language was not just a vehicle for the transmission of phonemes and hopefully many will agree that mythic themes (akin to the mythemes of Claude Lévi-Strauss) travelled down the ages too.

The formation of the Navan Research Group by Jim Mallory and others in 1986 and the appearance of its journal *Emania,* devoted to the study of the archaeological landscape and literary associations of Navan, were important developments in the multidisciplinary study of the royal sites in general. Equally significant was the Discovery Programme's survey of Tara initiated in 1991 under the direction of Conor Newman. It too was a multidisciplinary effort and its objective was to address the archaeological, historical and literary dimensions of this famous site. The major survey report on the hilltop complex and its broader landscape was published six years later. This and a comprehensive annotated bibliography of Tara that embraced the history, mythology and literary associations of this centre of pagan and medieval kingship was just the beginning of a programme of research that has fundamentally changed our understanding of 'Tara of the Kings'.[2] Its associations with the rituals of sacral kingship in myth and history indicate that some of its monuments were once the setting for spectacular ceremonies.

In a good illustration of myth illuminating archaeology, these kingly associations inspired Newman to re-evaluate the archaeological significance of the great linear earthwork known as the 'Banqueting Hall' since medieval times.[3] Aerial images of this monument give little sense of its scale and depth. In an imaginative interpretation of this enigmatic site he points out that it is both a ceremonial avenue that played a key part in kingly inaugurations and a semi-subterranean space (Fig. 1.3). When you stand within its two parallel earthen banks, you realise you cannot see over the banks which, of course, were once even higher. This is the one monument on the hill where views to the outside world are deliberately denied. Starting at the northern lower end, a visitor ascending gently to the hilltop, finds themselves in an enclosed space and, in an almost literal sense, enters Tara. As a processional way, however, it has other perplexing features – there are puzzling gaps in the banks on either side that from time to time allow a sight of the world outside.

Newman imagines a royal party slowly processing towards an inauguration ceremony in the summit sanctuary, the domain of the gods. Here the gaps in the banks have a crucial role to play for they offer glimpses of the burial mounds of the ancestral kings and queens of Tara on the right-hand side. One of these burial mounds is associated with a mythical king whose reign ended catastrophically. Reflecting on the lives of such ancestors, these monuments serve to remind a king-to-be of the burden of responsibility that comes with World Kingship, and of the fact that in re-enacting an inauguration ceremony he is about to take his place in history.

On the left-hand side, the Hill of Skreen is visible to the east. One of the famous legendary kings of Tara was banished to Skreen after being blinded by a bee sting, and because he was physically blemished he was disqualified from kingship. This is the limbo that awaits those who break the conventions of kingship. On the path to inauguration, the future king would reflect on the qualities and achievements of his mythic and historical predecessors and on the challenges and responsibilities he faced. This scenario is an excellent example of one way in which myth may be invoked to inspire fresh archaeological thinking.

Another instance is provided by the strange theme of asymmetry of form in some Irish tales.[4] In the story *Togail Bruidne Da Derga* (The Destruction of Da Derga's Hostel), a tale we will encounter again, a woman named Calib arrives at night demanding to enter the dwelling. She is of unprepossessing appearance to say the least with long black shins, pubic hair reaching to her knees, and her mouth is on one side of her head. She declares her many names – two of which are the names of war-goddesses – and is clearly from the Otherworld. She casts an evil eye on the assembled company and, standing on one leg and holding up one hand, she prophesizes the destruction to come.[5]

It is obviously a long leap from medieval Ireland to Iron Age Burgundy but here we have some evidence that supports the suggestion that the celebrated 'princess of Vix' was a woman who had a ritual role in society. She was buried with all the symbols of superior rank of the 5th century BC: a four-wheeled wagon, rich personal ornaments and a drinking set that included an immense bronze wine vessel capable of holding nearly 1100 litres made in a Greek colony in southern Italy. The female imagery on some of these objects is remarkable. Grotesque gorgons form the handles of the great vessel, a small statue of a veiled female stands in the centre of its lid, and images of Amazons decorate a Greek cup. These details and the fact that she was not physically distinguished, being of small stature (about five feet in height) and was marked by asymmetrical facial features and hip dysplasia that may have impaired her walking, have all prompted the proposition that she was a high-status ritualist with a role in the ceremonial serving of wine.

Another exceptional female burial of about AD 100 from Juellinge on the Danish island of Lolland was also accompanied by rich grave goods that included a bronze cauldron, a ladle, a wine-strainer, two glass beakers and two drinking horns. It is suggested she may also have had a role in drinking ceremonies. She too was lame having a deformity of her right leg caused by an osteochondroma, a large benign tumour on her thigh bone. Since both women may have had an important role in the sacramental serving of drink, it may be more than a coincidence that both were physically marked. The grotesque Calib is one of several figures who display asymmetry of posture (standing on one leg, raising one hand) or irregularity of bodily form (being one-eyed or lame) that are ritualistic traits in early Irish literature. If Irish tradition is any guide, a ritualist interpretation is increasingly likely for the women of Vix and Juellinge given their physical anomalies.⁶ A young woman interred in a tumulus in the townland of Farta, Co Galway, near the celebrated Turoe Stone in the west of Ireland, was also physically impaired (Chapter 7). She was accompanied by a horse burial and may have had a similar status, revered in life and venerated in death.

Sometimes archaeology may shed light on myth. Conor Newman's work affords yet another example. The 'sword in the stone' of Arthurian romance may well be the best known mythic theme today. It is certainly one of the most striking images in medieval legend not least because it echoes the motif in the 13th century Norse saga of the *Völsungs* in which the hero Sigmund draws the sword from a tree trunk, a dramatic subject immortalized by Richard Wagner in his *Der Ring des Nibelungen*.

The 'sword in the stone', however, is the story of the youthful Arthur who was able to pull a sword embedded in a stone to demonstrate that he was the legitimate king. Though not found in the early Welsh literature on Arthur, it does appear in Arthurian tales of the 13th century and later. While there are superficial resemblances between the Sigmund story and that of Arthur, other sources for this unusual and memorable motif have been proposed. It has even been traced back to the steppes of southern Russia where the Alans, a Sarmatian people, had a custom of plunging a naked sword in the earth – and then extracting it. Some of these folk found themselves in Roman legions and some settled in various places in the west, and their sword cult may have contributed an element to the Arthur story.⁷ There may be no single explanation for the tale but Newman has identified one piece of archaeological evidence that is very probably a part of its genesis.[8]

The Mullaghmast Stone is a decorated pillar now in the National Museum of Ireland. Its finely carved curvilinear motifs, including spirals and a triskele, are found on 6th century AD metalwork. Deep grooves, clearly later than some of the ornament, occur on several faces and appear to be marks created by repeatedly moving part of an iron blade to and fro in these narrow V-sectioned channels. The obvious conclusion that the stone was used as a sort of whetstone has been made before but Newman has identified a whole series of special or unusual stones that have also received this puzzling treatment.

Such blade marks – and sometimes areas of burnishing or polishing due to more orthodox blade sharpening – occur on a diverse group of important stones. These include a cross-inscribed pillar stone at Kilnasaggart, Co. Armagh, that has some 55 blade grooves incised near its base on its northern side and a memorial slab with an early Latin inscription from Penmachno, Gwynedd, north Wales, with several deep grooves near its base. A reused memorial slab from Roman Wroxeter in Shropshire with a 5th century inscription in Latinized primitive Irish, that includes the name Cunorix ('Hound King'), has one deep blade groove. Other significant stones nearing blade grooves include a number of ogham stones and high crosses. Over 30 blade marks are to be seen on the base of the high cross known as the Market Cross at Kells, Co. Meath, for instance, and this is not a case of medieval vandalism.

As Newman has shown, these and other iconic stones were deliberately selected for this treatment. While the polished areas, where they occur, are probably due to a normal lateral sharpening action, the grooves, used in a to-and-fro fashion, might sharpen the tip of a blade but would tend to blunt its edge. As he states 'the ostensibly contradictory actions that produced respectively the blade grooves and the burnished surfaces are reconcilable when visualised through the prism of ritual and ceremony'. The polished stone bestowed sharpness and potency to a sword while the grooves that blunted its edge symbolised the return of its potency to the stone. This symbiotic relationship between sacral stone and weapon, and the ritual act of drawing a blade across a stone, are probably two of a number of influences behind the unforgettable Arthurian motif.

Arthur's sword was forged in the Otherworld and it was to this place, to Avalon, that he was taken on his death. Britain still awaits the return of the once and future king from this mythical land. While Rathcroghan has an entrance to this mysterious place, its inhabitants, the *áes síde*, the people of the hollow hills, were ever present at Tara too. Because it was especially identified with the kingship of Ireland, it was a particular focus of supernatural threat. In one early tale, a king of Tara ascends the ramparts early in the morning accompanied by three druids and three seers to keep watch 'lest the men of the *síd* capture Ireland without his noticing'. In other words, he had to be vigilant in maintaining order and stability. This vigilance is expressed in one of the taboos or prohibitions of the kings of Tara in that it was forbidden for him to allow 'the sun to rise upon him as he lies in the plain of Tara'.[9] These prohibitions were a part of the contract between a sacred ruler and the Otherworld, for this world was the source of the power and authority of sacral kingship. If a king failed in his duties, or was unable to maintain cosmic order, the Otherworld might withdraw its favour with catastrophic consequences for all.

An examination of the requirements and rituals of the institution of sacral kingship in Irish tradition is a revealing exercise because the extensive literary evidence, studied by many scholars, has shown intriguing parallels with the ideology of kingship in Vedic India – implying a shared Indo-European heritage. We now understand that Tara, Rathcroghan and Navan were sacralized landscapes associated with the inauguration of sacred kings – and that is why they have Otherworldly associations. These were moments of profound ritual significance when the order of the world was re-established. These kings were world kings and their inauguration places were the centre of their world where there was a cosmic link between heaven and earth. A great timber pillar at Navan, revealed by archaeological excavation, and a sacred tree at Tara mentioned in an early medieval

Introduction

text, may have been expressions, in their different ways, of this tie between the supernatural and the natural worlds. Sacred trees too can be traced back to the Bronze Age.

The Irish evidence provides some clues as to what a prehistoric belief in an Otherworld might entail. The medieval literature also offers some indication of the ceremonial that may have been a part of pagan rites of kingship. Since there is now general archaeological agreement that ritual is a human practice that leaves material traces, that it 'extends from the local, informal and ephemeral to the public and highly organized'[10] archaeologists should be alert to the possibility that the complex symbolic actions in this area may be identifiable in the archaeological record. The use of Irish analogues may even encourage consideration of questions of cosmology. Of course, not everyone would agree that medieval texts can shed light on a prehistoric past centuries or even millennia before. There are even those who prefer to see this great literary corpus as a wholly medieval construct.[11] This belief, however, is quite untenable for there are ancient mythic themes to be explored as we shall see.

CHAPTER 1

The Invented Past

In the 8th century tale *Táin Bó Fraích* (The Cattle Raid of Fraoch) there is a grandiose description of the house of Ailill and Medb in the rath or fort of Crúachain:

> This was the arrangement of the house: seven partitions in it, seven beds from the fire to the wall in the house all around. There was a fronting of bronze on each bed, carved red yew all covered with fair varied ornament. Three rods of bronze at the step of each bed. Seven rods of copper from the centre of the floor to the ridge-pole of the house. The house was built of pine. A roof of slates was on it outside. There were sixteen windows in it, and a shutter of copper for each of them. There was a lattice of copper across the skylight. Four pillars of copper were over the bed of Ailill and Medb which stood in the middle of the house all adorned with bronze. Two borders of gilded silver were around it. A silver stave reached from the border to the cross-beams of the house. It ran round the house from one door to the other ....[1]

Another fanciful account of Rathcroghan's royal house occurs in *Fled Bricrenn* (Bricriu's Feast). Here it has twelve windows 'with glass in the openings' and 'room for the hosts of valiant heroes' of Ulster who are visiting Rathcroghan.[2] Like the description of Conchobar's kingly house at Emain Macha (Navan Fort), this would seem to be an instance where a place associated with pagan kingly ceremonial was reinvented as a splendid royal residence in medieval times. A large circular mound, Rathcroghan Mound, is traditionally believed to be the site of Queen Medb's royal establishment. However, detailed geophysical survey has demonstrated that this mound was probably

1. The Invented Past

an elaborate ceremonial centre with a long and protracted prehistory. This broad flat-topped circular mound, with an average basal diameter of 89 m and a height of some 5.5 m is the focal monument standing in the centre of a complex of burial mounds, enclosures and other monuments. The latter include a very large linear earthwork, pillar stones and that enigmatic entrance to the Otherworld, today popularly known as Úaimh na gCat or Oweynagat ('the cave of the cats').

We now know that the great mound lies in the approximate centre of a great circular enclosure barely visible on the ground. It is about 360 m in diameter and is formed by a substantial ditch (Fig. 1.1). Other monuments within this large circle include two conjoined ring barrows on the east and a northern enclosure approached by a processional avenue. These linear features probably contained timber palisades and are similar to the smaller avenues that lead to circular enclosures at Navan which have been dated to the later centuries BC. The huge mound was also approached via a ceremonial way on its eastern side and was contained by a timber palisade. Intensively surveyed using a range of geophysical techniques, it is evident that it contains a number of circular structures including a large penannular enclosure about 22 m across. There are traces of a radial design on its summit formed by shallow depressions dividing the surface in a segmented fashion. A circular structure formed by a double ring of timber posts may once have stood on its summit too. Several details in this suite of geophysical analyses, including the radial lines and the entombment of circular structures with a mound, invite comparison with the excavation results from Navan Fort.[3]

The story of Dathi's Mound offers another mismatch between text and archaeology at Rathcroghan. This is a burial mound a short distance south of the great focal monument (Fig. 1.2). It is an Iron Age ring barrow with a pillar stone on a low central mound that is surrounded by a bank with internal ditch. Limited excavation in the 1980s provided some radiocarbon dates that suggested it was constructed in the last century BC or the early centuries AD.[4] As its name indicates, however, it has been traditionally believed to be the burial place of one Dathi or Nath Í. He was supposedly the last pagan

12   *Myth and Materiality*

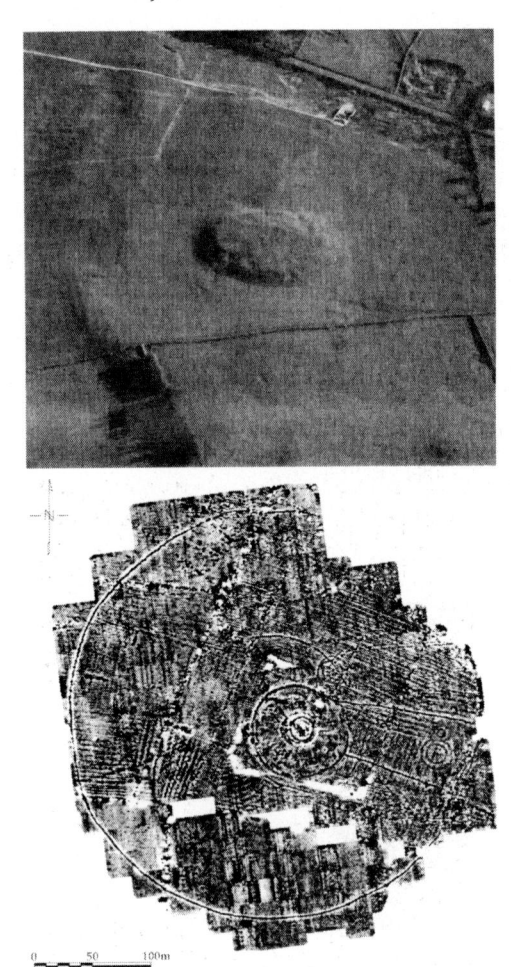

Figure 1.1. Rathcroghan Mound and the results of geophysical survey. Magnetic gradiometry has disclosed a series of sub-surface features in its immediate vicinity. The great mound is clearly defined in the centre of the image and has various structures entombed within it. On the east it is approached by a trapezoidal avenue in which two burial mounds are visible. Immediately to the north, a northern enclosure has its own eastern avenue. All these features are encircled by a very large ditched enclosure 360 m in diameter.

1. *The Invented Past* 13

Figure 1.2. Above. A 19th century drawing of Dathi's Mound at Rathcroghan. Below. 'The bier of King Dathi carried in the Alps' from John Boyle O'Reilly's Irish Songs and Ballads (1888).

king of Ireland who died in the middle of the 5th century AD. In the tale *Aided Nath Í ocus a adnacol* (The Death of Nath Í and his burial), preserved in the 12th century Lebor na hUidre, we are told how he and his warriors undertake a military expedition to *Sliab nElpa*. Here he attacks the tower of a Christian king named Formenus who prays to God to bring an end to the reign of Dathi. God sides with Formenus and the misfortunate Dathi is struck dead by lightning. His corpse is carried back to Ireland and buried in Rathcroghan (Fig. 1.2).

Elpa is the Irish name for the Alps and this suggestion of an early Irish military foray to the Continent was recounted by later writers in the 16th and 17th centuries. The story was particularly popular in the 19th century as an example of early Ireland's military capabilities. One romantic writer, following manuscript clues, even claimed to have traced the warrior-king's journey to the region of Bad Ragaz at the foot of the Swiss Alps where it seemed Formenus may have had his tower.[5] Of course this was at a time when the historical accuracy of these medieval texts was widely accepted – but there was no Irish invasion of Switzerland in the 5th century. If the shadowy Dathi ever ventured abroad, he probably led a raiding party to Alba (Britain – the Classical Albion) and his legend rests on medieval embellishment and scribal confusion.[6] Sadly for him, Dathi was eclipsed as the emblematic Celtic warrior by Cú Chulainn towards the end of the 19th century. All this more recent myth-making is not be scorned however – the 19th and early 20th century was a time when a romantic nationalism made use of the past to create a future.

Medieval invention and exaggeration are part of the story of Tara too. The earliest accounts of the sites on this famous hill were compiled for political reasons to enhance the claims of the southern Uí Néill to the kingship of Tara. One text *Dindgnai Temrach* (The Remarkable Places of Tara) is attributed to the Uí Néill court poet Cúán úa Lothcháin. In this and other writings, its monuments were linked to mythical ancestral figures or kings such as Cormac mac Airt, the greatest of Tara's kings who supposedly ruled in the 2nd or 3rd century AD, and Niall Noígiallach (Niall of the Nine Hostages – so named because he was supposed to have taken hostages at nine

1. The Invented Past

locations in Ireland and abroad). Written around AD 1000, this medieval archaeological survey is an unusually detailed description of the monuments on the hill compiled from a quite careful examination of the sites visible at the time and following a route from south to north. George Petrie and John O'Donovan used it in their efforts to correlate the visible archaeological remains with the literary evidence some eight centuries later in 1836 in the course of their work for the Ordnance Survey. The medieval names for some of the monuments are those in use today (Fig. 3.1).[7]

That linear earthwork they called the Banqueting Hall is one of the more prominent grassy monuments at the northern end of the hilltop. It is formed by a pair of slightly curving but parallel earthen banks set some 23 m apart and 203 m in length. There are gaps in each bank at irregular intervals, perhaps eleven in total. As already mentioned, it is an imposing processional way that could well have played an important role in the rituals that were a part of entering Tara's sacred precincts as Newman has shown (Fig. 1.3). However the 11th century account just mentioned describes it (in Petrie and O'Donovan's translation) as follows:

> Long na m-ban, *i.e.* Teach Midhchuarta, is to the north-west of the eastern mound. The ruins of this house are situate thus: the lower part to the north and the higher part to the south; and walls are raised about it to the east and to the west. The northern side of it is enclosed and small; the lie of it is north and south. It is in the form of a long house, with twelve doors upon it, or fourteen, seven to the west, and seven to the east. It is said, that it was here the Feis Teamhrach was held, which seems true; because as many men would fit in it as would form the choice part of the men of Ireland. And this was the great house of a thousand soldiers.

Elsewhere it is identified as the *tech midchúarta* or house of the mead-circuit of Cormac mac Airt and several texts are devoted to describing the complex formal seating arrangements according to rank and vocation in the great banqueting hall. These were sketched by a scribe in the 12th century Book of Leinster and in the later Yellow

Figure 1.3. The 'Banqueting Hall' on the Hill of Tara. The human figures give an idea of its scale and the present height of its earthen banks. One of the gaps in the banks of the linear earthwork is visible on the right. The hole on the lower left is due to quarrying.

Book of Lecan (Fig. 1.4). The rectangular form of the great hall seemed to broadly agree with the shape of the rectilinear earthwork and the notion that it was indeed the famed banqueting hall survived well into the 20th century. In 1919 Macalister produced a reconstruction and a plan of the internal arrangements of a great aisled timber rectangular building of truly heroic proportions with separate booths for the different participants. It was about 23 m wide and over 200 m long. He did note that its dimensions recalled those of Solomon's Temple in ancient Jerusalem but still believed the correspondence in size with the visible earthwork was important supportive evidence.[8]

There is no doubt that the seating plan in a king's hall in early Ireland reflected social status as indeed did the apportioning of different cuts of meat. But these buildings were probably circular and, like the literary depictions of the great houses of Ailill and Medb and Conchobar, they were probably richly decorated. However the

1. The Invented Past 17

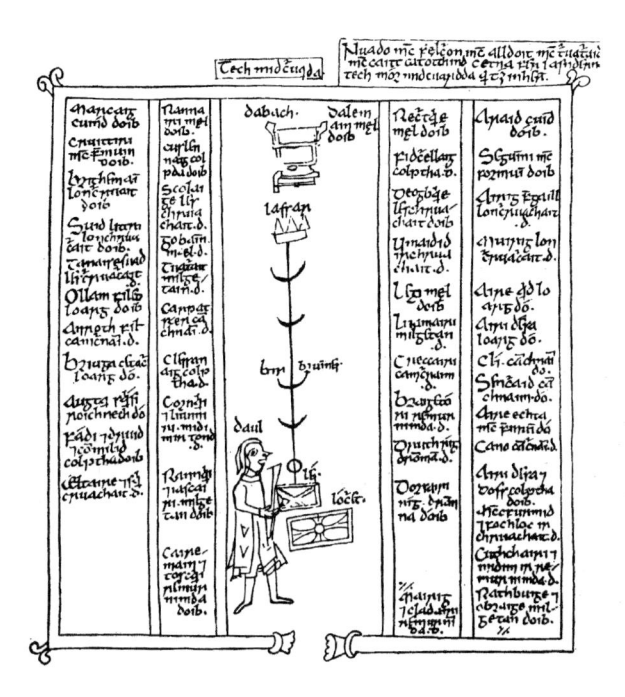

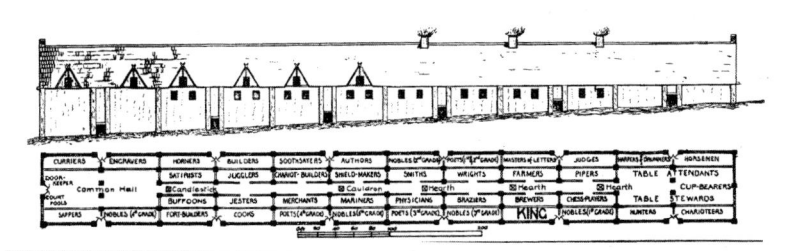

Figure 1.4. Above. A drawing of the great Banqueting Hall on the Hill of Tara based on the representation in the 12th century Book of Leinster. Below. R. A. S. Macalister's 1919 reconstruction of a 200 m long Banqueting Hall based on the dimensions of the linear earthwork on the hill.

descriptions that have come down to us have many sources and are a marvellous mix of native, imaginary and Classical detail.

Medieval writers imagined Conchobar's royal house at Emain Macha as a place of prodigious hospitality where enormous quantities of drink were consumed.[9] It is described in extravagant terms in the tale *Tochmarc Emire* (The Wooing of Emer) and was supposedly built like the great mead hall on Tara:

> There lived once upon a time a great and famous king in Emain Macha, whose name was Conchobar, son of Fachtna Fathach. In his reign there was much store of good things enjoyed by the men of Ulster. Peace there was, and quiet, and pleasant greeting; there were fruits and fatness and harvest of the sea; there was power and law and good lordship during his time among the men of Erin. In the king's house at Emain was great state and rank and plenty. On this wise was that house, the Red Branch of Conchobar, namely, after the likeness of the Tech Midchuarta of Tara. Nine compartments were in it from the fire to the wall. Thirty feet was the height of each bronze partition in the house. Carvings of red yew therein. A wooden floor beneath, and a roofing of tiles above. The compartment of Conchobar was in the front of the house, with a ceiling of silver with pillars of bronze. Their headpieces glittered with gold and were set with carbuncles, so that day and night were equally light therein ....[10]

Edel Bhreathnach's assessment of this account is to the point:

> This fanciful description fits the mythical and heroic flavour of the tale and draws on many sources: imaginary, Classical, and contemporary accounts of Carolingian royal apartments, possibly the elevated royal thrones which were features at palaces at Aachen or Ingelheim. It may owe something to accounts of luxurious objects in precious metal and gems that were part of Irish and Carolingian royal treasures. The cultural milieu of Conchobar's apartment, therefore, is medieval and is unlikely to have drawn on knowledge of the structures or seating arrangements of prehistoric Emain.[11]

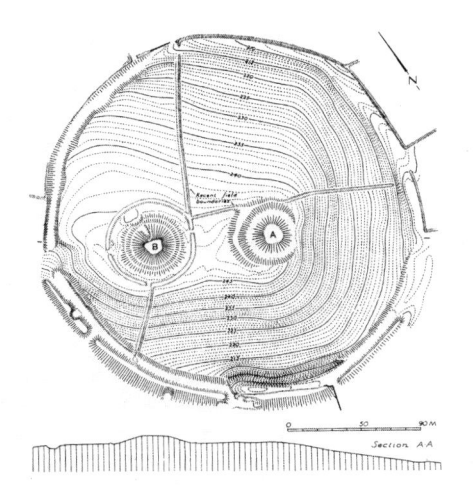

Figure 1.5. Above. Plan of Navan Fort showing the large mound (Site B) and the location of Site A (now A-C) to the right (© Crown DfC). Below. An artist's impression of Navan Fort today, the great mound is on the left.

Once again the literary evidence and the archaeology do not agree. Various excavations and geophysical surveys at Navan Fort have provided quite a good picture of at least part of its prehistoric story.[12] A summary of these investigations illustrates the discrepancy between medieval romance and archaeological reality. This great earthwork is a large circle formed by a wide deep ditch with a very substantial external earthen bank (Fig. 1.5). An oak timber recovered from excavation of the lowest fill of the ditch has provided a dendrochronological felling date of 94 ± 9 BC.[13] So the enclosure may have been built shortly

20 *Myth and Materiality*

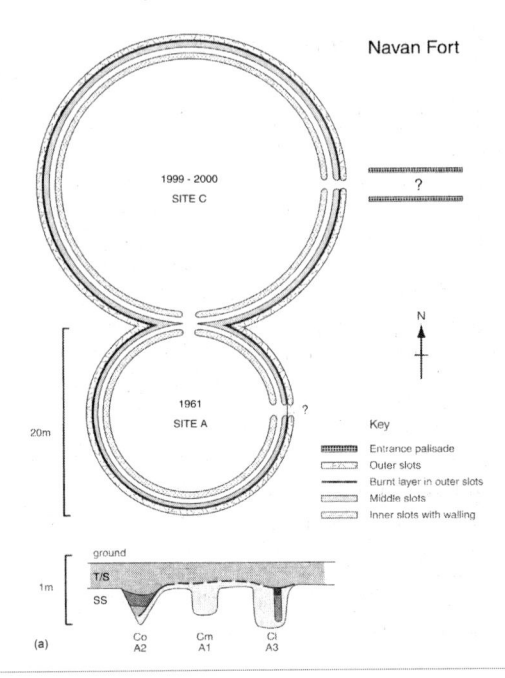

Figure 1.6a. Schematic plan of Navan Site A-C: the palisade trenches are now known to form a succession of large figure-of-eight structures.

before this, around 100 BC, and may be broadly contemporary with Ráth na Rí on Tara.

Early excavations in the interior were conducted at two visible monuments: a low circular mound called Site A and at a very large circular flat-topped mound nearby called Site B. Thanks to the excavations at Site A in 1961 and subsequent investigations there and at a conjoined site (Site C) revealed by geophysical survey over 30 years later we now know this was originally a large and complex monument some 50 m across. It has a significant bearing on the interpretation of the discoveries at the great mound nearby (Site B) as we shall see.

Site A–C, as it is now called, consists of two components that form a figure-of-eight plan (Fig. 1.6), each essentially consisting of three concentric trenches. A series of post-holes, 1 m apart on average,

1. *The Invented Past*

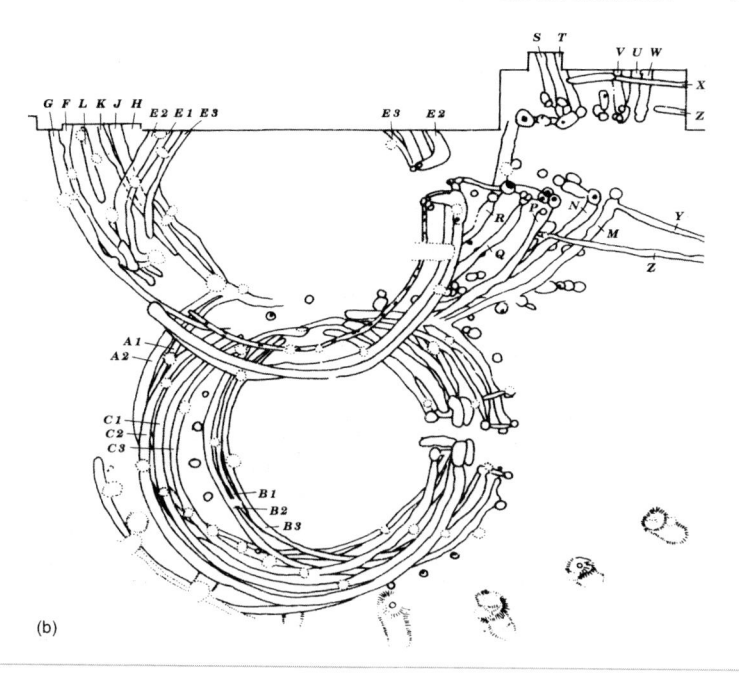

Figure 1.6b. The complex sequence of circular enclosures (Phases 3ii–3iii) at Navan Site B pre-dating the 40m structure (Phase 4). Some of these form figure-of-eight structures and some have approach ways on the east. Several of the pits of the earlier timber circle (Phase 3i) are visible on the lower right.

was identified in the innermost trench indicating that some form of timber walling had been embedded in it. A sequence was established showing that the middle trench was dug first, then the outer and finally the inner and it seemed that each trench was used in turn independently of the others. Therefore it was suggested that the three circles represent successive timber structures. Limited excavation revealed that the inner timber structure has been burnt in situ. Large quantities of burnt pig and cattle bones were recovered, so much in fact that the deliberate cremation of these animals was considered a possibility. Radiocarbon dates indicate that Site A–C was probably contemporary with the great timber structure at nearby Site B (Phase 4) dated to the last century BC.

The sheer size of these circles, from about 16.5 m to over 30 m in diameter, with no evidence of any internal timber supports, implies they were not roofed and a ceremonial purpose seems undeniable. This phase of activity was followed by another circular timber structure, formed by pair of concentric ring slots with diameters of about 12 m and 16 m, and the subsequent construction of a low barrow with ditch and external bank of uncertain date.

The large mound (Site B), some 6 m high and 50 m in diameter, was excavated between 1963 and 1971. About two thirds of the site were examined and after excavation the mound was restored to its original form. Five major phases were identified. Phases 1–2 represented early prehistoric activity there while Phase 3 represents the major period of later prehistoric activity and is divided into three sub-phases (3i–3iii). In Phase 3i, a circular ditch surrounded a ring of spaced timber posts probably dating to the earlier centuries of the 1st millennium BC. This was the primary sacred circle, replicated again and again in the centuries to follow. Phases 3ii–3iii probably date from the 4th to the 2nd century BC.

Phase 3ii is represented by an extraordinary complex sequence of circular timber structures revealed as foundation trenches. A series of nine successive trenches overlay the line of the presumed timber circle of Phase 3i on the south (Fig. 1.6). The foundation trenches more or less occurred in three groups of three concentric circles (A1–2, B1–3, C1–3) and the sequence in each group was middle, outer and inner (as observed at Site A–C). Small burnt areas and groups of flat stones indicated the presence of hearths at the centres of these circular structures. Attached to or touching the northern side of the southern A, B and C trenches was a series of six further foundation trenches of greater diameter. Individual elements of the northern and southern ring slot groups were evidently attached and formed figure-of-eight units.

It seems that the southern trenches of these figure-of-eight structures represented the walls of eight or nine successive round houses with doors on the east, most of them communicating with other enclosures on the north, these in turn being approached by fenced approach ways. With the presence of hearths and what seemed to be occupation debris including animal bone and sherds of coarse pottery, it was reasonable to consider these to have been domestic dwellings with attached stock-yards entered via droveways. Other finds were unusual and included shale armlets, glass beads, a bronze bar toggle, part of a socketed bronze sickle, and the skull and jaw of a Barbary Ape *(Macaca sylvanus)*.

The recognition that the larger figure-of-eight structures at Site A–C could never have been roofed has suggested that these Site B circles may have been primarily non-utilitarian.[14] That ritual may have been a significant part of the activities in these structures seems very likely particularly given the exceptional repetitive constructional sequence. Phase 3iii represents yet another series of three ring slots to the north (E1–3) that display the same sequential pattern. The developments that follow in Phases 4 and 5 were entirely ritual in nature and must give weight to the likelihood that there was a major ritual component throughout all the preceding stages of Phase 3 as well.

The subsequent history of the site was undoubtedly ceremonial in quite an exceptional way. Phase 4 is represented by the construction of a huge multi-ring timber structure (Fig. 6.4). It was circular and consisted of five major concentric rings of posts and a large central post. The entrance was on the west and here the internal post-ring system was interrupted by four roughly parallel rows of posts forming three aisles leading to the centre of the structure. At the centre was a timber post so large that it had to be dragged at an angle into its post-pit on a sloping ramp 6 m long cut into subsoil. It could have been 13 m or more in height.

There were no hearths or other evidence for occupation in this 40 m structure and dendrochronological analysis has determined that the large central post was felled in late 95 BC or early 94 BC. This dates the completion of this remarkable building. Phase 5 followed quickly and the multi-ring structure evidently had a relatively short period of use. While it was still standing, its interior was filled with a cairn of limestone boulders. That the wooden structure still stood was demonstrated by the survival of roughly cylindrical vertical voids left by its rotted oak posts at a high level in the cairn. Its surface was divided into clearly-defined but somewhat irregular radial sectors by the use of different sizes of stones, by various arrangements of stones and by varying admixtures of soil, clay or turf in the sectors. The radial divisions visible in the top of the cairn did not apparently extend downwards through the cairn but they did have the central pillar as their focal point. The cairn was finally covered by a mound of turves and much of this material must have been obtained by stripping the turf and topsoil from a large area.

It is not unreasonable to see this edifice as a great timber temple or shrine completely at variance with the literary image of Emain Macha. Indeed Jim Mallory has described the latter picture as the 'standard Irish palace description'. In an exhaustive study of the material world of these medieval writings he has shown that helpful correspondences with the Iron Age archaeological evidence are rare indeed particularly when generic correlations are excluded – chariots being a ubiquitous feature of heroic societies for instance. He was the first to demonstrate how the swords described in the epic *Táin Bó Cúailnge* (The Cattle Raid of Cooley or simply the *Táin*) far from being La Tène type weapons, were comparable to swords of the Viking era. In other words, the swords of these epic stories are the swords familiar to the medieval tellers of these tales.[15]

This was probably a deliberate technique akin to the visual anachronism so familiar in medieval and Renaissance art – as where Apollo might be depicted in medieval dress.[16] The introduction of familiar traits offered a medieval Irish audience a measure of convincing truthfulness. It also served to occlude parts of a pagan past that was still remembered because, of course, in medieval times the past was there to illustrate the power of God. This was not a strategy based on absolute ignorance for there was a rich antiquarian tradition in Ireland at the time and some medieval writers were certainly acquainted with older antiquities. For example, the *Annals of Lough Cé* in the year 1191 record a number of archaeological finds from the River Corrib, once known as the Gaillimh or Galway river: 'the Gaillimh became dry this year, and an axe was found in it measuring a hand from one point of it to the other, and a spear was found in it, and the breadth of the blade of this spear was three hands and three fingers; and its length was a hand from the shoulder'. There are even some tantalizing hints of an antiquarian curiosity that occasionally extended beyond literary explanation and speculation to the deliberate exploration of ancient remains.[17]

Nonetheless, the 'window on the Iron Age' now seems firmly closed. This well-known phrase was popularized by the Celtic scholar K. H. Jackson in 1964 when he argued that some Irish medieval literature, and in particular the Ulster Cycle, depicted a pre-Christian Iron Age world. For him, the *Táin* with its heroic warriors and endemic warfare did depict a genuine Iron Age even though many of the individuals represented were not historical figures. The fact that archaeological excavations at Navan Fort between 1963 and 1972 revealed that this was a great ritual centre in the Iron Age rather than a fortified royal court probably marked the beginning of the slow demolition of Jackson's thesis. These discoveries were considered evidence of a total disassociation between prehistoric archaeology and medieval text. For Aitchison, Navan Fort constituted the physical remains of the past while Emain Macha represented the constructed, part mythological, part ideological, past.[18]

The rich heritage of saga, legal and genealogical literature was also subjected to critical scrutiny, demonstrating that the Christian church and Classical learning had had a much greater impact on this material than had been supposed. It was argued that all of this great body of medieval literature was the product of a monastic milieu that presented a version of a past that was profoundly transformed if not actually created by Christian writers. With great erudition, a number of fierce philologists and dogmatic historians effectively created a new and influential orthodoxy in which pre-Christian traditions had a minimal role to play.

The terms nativist and anti-nativist gradually entered the lexicon of Celtic studies, those of an anti-nativist or revisionist persuasion questioned any significant contribution by an older oral tradition to medieval texts, viewing them as original compositions created *de novo* in a Christian environment. One writer has even suggested some of this number must have feared the potent force of stories rich in emotional and symbolic power, retreating into a merely linguistic or historical analysis.[19] To be fair, Celtic studies has been well served by many scholars who toiled like William Cowper's 'learn'd philologists, who chase a panting syllable through time and space'.[20] Fortunately there were those who did not neglect the mythological content of the narrative literature and in recent decades enormous advances have been made by Celtic scholars like Proinsias Mac Cana, Tomás Ó Cathasaigh, John Carey and many others.

Today there is a greater understanding of the interactive and mutually influential character of both oral and written genres in early medieval Ireland.[21] As Ó Cathasaigh has written 'early Irish literature is not the detritus of a lost mythology, nor yet a new phenomenon, born, like Athena, fully grown. It is the creation of a society which had two sets of cultural institutions, one indigenous, and oral in its medium, the other ecclesiastical and literate. These were sometimes hostile, sometimes amicable, but between them they contributed to the formation of a literature which combined matter drawn from the oral tradition with other elements and transmuted them into something new'.[22]

There is also a greater appreciation of the significance of the mythological content of this material even though, ironically, Jackson was guarded about the study of myth. The mythological content of the medieval literary tradition in Ireland and Wales was, he thought, just 'a gold-mine for the speculation of scholars' and could be 'tailored to fit anything, and hence they are a favourite device in the hands of the unscholarly'.[23] In his study of the 'window on the Iron Age' he did not engage with mythology.

It seems very likely that in creating an impressive image of an heroic past for their medieval audience, a world peopled by intrepid warriors and illustrious kings who lived in splendidly decorated dwellings like Navan, the Christian authors were also anxious to obscure the potent pagan symbolism linked to the rituals performed at these great ceremonial centres. Yet paradoxically, it was this primordial past that might also lend support to claims of political legitimacy and antiquity, and this was a very good reason to include some mythic credentials. This was a narrative strategy to claim an immemorial authority and to alert an audience to deeper significant meanings.

Most archaeologists would probably be familiar with the historical school of thought in which ancient myth may be thought to hold some age-old truths. The discovery of Troy and Mycenae by Heinrich Schliemann and Knossos by Arthur Evans are simple examples of this in the Mediterranean world. But for many archaeologists working in western and northern Europe the very term myth is a likely reminder of the problematic nature of any engagement between the material and the immaterial and inevitably raises the question of the reliability of medieval tales to shed any light on the distant past. It must recall some of those numerous instances where myth and archaeology have converged in a very suspect way. Jackson's qualms were not entirely unfounded.

One obvious example is Plato's story of Atlantis, that fabled island in the outer ocean beyond the Rock of Gibraltar, the Pillars of Hercules, and his account of its destruction by earthquake and flood. This is a myth that has captured the imagination of scholars and lunatics alike. Since the 19th century, the Atlantis myth has spawned a vast and diverse literature and, sadly, Ireland can be said to be partly to blame. The remarkable Ignatius Donnelly, an American politician of Irish parentage, described as 'perhaps the most erudite man ever to sit in the House of Representatives', may be credited with initiating a school of archaeological speculation that continues to this day. Citing a wide and bizarre range of archaeological material from around the world, and early Irish legend, and much else besides, he argued that the Americas, ancient Egypt and Ireland had been colonized at an early date by highly civilized Atlanteans, as he called them, from this lost continent.

His book *Atlantis: the Antediluvian World*, first published in 1882, is widely accepted as the modern inspiration for a pseudo-science that continues to attract numerous followers.[24] In uncritically comparing material from many different places and many different periods, Donnelly engaged in an unsound methodological exercise that is still very much at home in the weird and wonderful world of pseudo-archaeology in which monuments, artistic motifs or myths are compared to each other without any regard for their respective contexts.[25] This is not a benign and eccentric form of popularization, however, for it trivializes an archaeology that aims to illuminate aspects of our common humanity.

Of course, the quest has continued unabated. Just to cite two quite different examples – of many hundreds in more recent times – the Classical scholar John Victor Luce contended in the 1960s that the destruction of Atlantis was a tale ultimately based on the Bronze Age volcanic eruption of the island of Santorini.[26] This proposal has been rejected by a French archaeologist who maintains that a former island now below sea level northwest of Cape Spartel on the Moroccan coast, near Tangier and south-west of the Strait of Gibraltar, was the location of the mythical realm. This submarine mud bank seems a rather modest location for the mythical cities of the kings of Atlantis.[27]

In examining tales in medieval Irish texts, we are on surer ground employing comparative mythology that, in an Irish context, involves the identification of shared mythic themes in different Indo-European traditions. In many instances, however, we will find ourselves dealing not so much with coherent themes but with remnants of myths fortuitously preserved. In today's world, truth for many is to be found in scientific rationality, not in myth or even in religion. Yet myths once made sense of the past – either in explanatory or symbolic terms – and survived because they carried a historically authoritative meaning that resonated with successive generations.

CHAPTER 2

The Mythic Past

A 9th century Irish manuscript preserved in the monastery of St Gall in Switzerland has a short poem inscribed in its margin by an Irish monk. It reads 'Bitter is the wind tonight, It tosses the ocean's white hair, Tonight I fear not the fierce warriors of Norway, Coursing on the Irish sea.'[1] These few lines were probably written in a coastal monastery like Nendrum in Co. Down when Viking raiders posed an ever present threat. It was a multitude of monastic scribes like this anonymous individual who, in more peaceful times, wrote down an enormous corpus of native lore and conserved it for posterity. Ironically, it was these fearsome Northmen who colonized Iceland and their descendants left another legacy that preserved a great part of the mythology of the Nordic world. The Icelandic texts were written in a medieval Christian context too and the 13th century *Prose Edda,* for example, contains many of the famous tales of gods and heroes and of the creation and destruction of the world that many centuries later would inspire the operas of Richard Wagner and Tolkien's *The Lord of the Rings.*

The surviving corpus of early Irish texts incorporates a large body of narrative literature that includes the epic *Táin Bó Cúailnge*. This is a story of a great *táin bó* or cattle raid and it tells of an invasion of Ulster by a great army led by Medb and Ailill, those rulers of Connacht whose court was at Rathcroghan in Co. Roscommon. Their aim was to seize a celebrated brown bull, the Donn Cúailnge, from the Cooley peninsula in Co. Louth, so that Medb will have a bull to match the great white-horned bull, the Findbennach, owned by her husband. The story also tells of the heroic defense of the province of Ulster by the legendary warrior Cú Chulainn who has many mythic aspects and who, as we learn in another tale, had a divine father, namely the great Celtic god Lug. Cú Chulainn's attributes include some fabulous weaponry and a remarkable capacity for battle-frenzy, and presumably these are just some of the mythic elements in the tale that did not impress one monastic scribe who penned a version of the story in the late 12th century. He was compelled to add a final comment in Latin to this second recension of the tale: 'But I who have written this story or rather fable do not give credence to the various incidents related in it. For some things in it are the deceptions of demons, others poetic fiction; some are probable, others improbable; while others are for the amusement of foolish people'.[2] He may, however, have appreciated the rather peculiar ending to the epic.

The *Táin* ends with a lengthy battle between the two bulls in which they traverse the whole of Ireland. The titanic struggle begins at Rathcroghan where a man named Bricriu mac Garbada, described as a most fair-minded person, was chosen to be an eyewitness to the battle. Caught between the fighting animals he was trampled to death. The Donn Cúailnge is the eventual victor. Passing Rathcroghan with the mangled remains of Ailill's prize bull on his horns, he scatters the body parts of the Findbennach in various places across Ireland before reaching his homeland in Cooley, Co. Louth, where, in his fury, he slaughters some of its inhabitants before collapsing and dying. The ending runs as follows with the coming of the brown bull to Rathcroghan:

> The Donn Cúailnge arrived. He turned his right side to Crúachu and left there a heap of the liver of the Findbennach. Whence the name Crúachna Áe. He came forward to the brink of Áth Mór and there he left the loin of the Findbennach. Whence the name Áth Luain. He came eastwards into the land of Meath to Áth Troim and there he left the liver of the Findbennach. He tossed his head fiercely and shook off the Findbennach over Ireland. He threw his thigh as far as Port Lárge. He threw his rib-cage as far as Dublind which is called Áth Clíath. After that he faced towards the north and recognised the land of Cúailnge and came towards it ....[3]

The dismembered parts of the defeated Connacht bull create or are linked to features of the Irish landscape. Some parts of its liver are left at Rathcroghan. Its loin is deposited at the great ford called Áth Luain, the ford of the haunch, modern Athlone. The rest of the liver is left at a ford on the sacred river Boyne at Trim in Co. Meath, a thigh lands in Waterford and the rib-cage in Dublin. This is a distorted reflection, it would seem, of elements of an Indo-European myth of creation where the theme of dismemberment figures in naming or origin legends. According to Proinsias Mac Cana this motif recalls the Indian story of the god Śiva who wanders with the body of his beloved wife Satī on his shoulder until the other gods enter the dead body and dispose of it bit by bit. The places where the pieces fall become shrines of the mother goddess. It has also been compared to an Indo-Iranian creation myth that tells of the creation of the world through the primordial sacrifice of a man and a bull or an ox. The puzzling simultaneous deaths of Bricriu and the Findbennach may be an echo of another Indo-European myth that involved the sacrifice of a man and a bull in the creation of the world, an act that established a pattern for all future sacrifice and all future creation.[4]

In composing this strange apotheosis to the epic, the author drew on strands of ancient myths to offer a compelling metaphor for the struggle between Connacht and Ulster that elevated this conflict to a quasi-mythical level and, with the death of both animals, offered a striking image of the utter futility of war to his medieval audience.[5] This point may well have been appreciated by that sceptical scribe.

The redoubtable Queen Maeve of the *Táin*, Medb of Crúachain, appears in that saga as a capricious war-leader in the quest for the brown bull. She is the dominating partner in a marriage in which Ailill is presented as a compliant spouse tolerant of her promiscuity. Her sexual capacity is apparent in other tales as well, as in her declaration that 'I never was without one man in the shadow of another', and in the fact that she had at least four husbands, Ailill being the last.[6] In the early 20th century, Medb's behaviour was seen as an illustration of the licentiousness and moral laxity of pagan times but as one writer memorably put it 'this is one of the not infrequent instances where bad morals make good mythology'.⁷ This Medb of medieval times was not a historical person and her promiscuity is an echo of an older and much more significant mythic figure. 'In early Ireland women were not sovereigns, but sovereignty was conceived of as female'.⁸

The original Medb was a goddess of sovereignty who was the personification of the land. Her name is cognate with words in Irish and other languages associated with drink (like the English word 'mead'). It has been variously taken to mean 'the drunken one', 'she who intoxicates' or 'she who belongs to the mead'. The name of this divine dispenser of liquor may have had the added attraction of ambiguity because while the association with drink and mead (*medhw-o-*) is generally acknowledged, there may also be an allusion to one who rules or commands (*med-wo-*).⁹ There is an Indo-European dimension to this motif of an intoxicating goddess associated with fertility and human kingship. Georges Dumézil saw a connection in both name and function between this Medb and the beautiful Mādhavī of the great Indian epic the Mahabharata. She was gifted with the ability to become a virgin after childbirth and provided sons for a succession of world kings ensuring the continuation of their royal lineage. Her name is a derivative of the Indo-European *medhu-* (mead) and Dumézil argued that it could mean 'the intoxicating one'.¹⁰

Another noteworthy confrontation of epic proportions in early literature is one between the pagan gods of Ireland found in two versions of *Cath Maige Tuired* (The Battle of Moytura). According to Irish tradition there were two battles, one supposedly at Cong in Co. Mayo, the second at what is now Moytirra, Co. Sligo.¹¹ The latter would appear to be the original conflict, one between the Tuatha Dé Danann (the people of the goddess Danu) and the Fomoiri (a name that may mean the people from beneath the sea). This great battle is a variation on the theme of the war of the gods well known in Nordic and Greek myth. It has been compared to the combat between the Asuras and Devas in Vedic India and that between the Aesir and Vanir in Scandinavian mythology. There are various contests but the main engagement in a complex tale is the combat between the pan-Celtic god Lug (whose name figures, for instance, in the ancient name of

Lyon – Lugdunum) and the monstrous Balor of the evil eye who he slays with a sling-shot. The battle then becomes a rout and the Fomoiri are driven back to the sea. Peace is proclaimed but the last words are chanted by the war-goddess the Morrígan who prophesizes the end of the world foretelling the evils that will occur then:

> I shall not see a world that will be dear to me
> Summer without blossoms
> Cattle will be without milk
> Women without modesty
> Men without valor
> Conquests without a king ....

Aside from Lug, other participants in this epic include the mythical kings Nuadu and Bres. Each of these reflect a different aspect of the requirements of the institution of sacral kingship (Chapter 3): Lug is physically perfect, all-knowing and master of all the arts, Bres delivers a false judgment amongst other misdeeds and is a flawed king, while Nuadu loses an arm and this physical blemish disqualifies him from the kingship until he is given a silver replacement. In this respect the story is an exemplary myth embodying in a dramatic way the ideology and values of the community and exemplifying some of the positive values of society as to how lives should be lived.[12]

It is the mythological content of this early Irish literature that may shed light on prehistoric beliefs and practices. Not everyone would agree of course – and sometimes for good reasons. There is a huge chronological gap between medieval text and prehistoric activity and it may be difficult to distinguish between literary invention and a genuine archaism. Of course, some of these myths were invented but more often than not pre-existing material was reutilized or distorted by Christian scribes in a monastic context. There is an interesting parallel here with the actions of the forerunners of these Irish scribes who wrote the Christian gospels and who also were content to include fragments of older eastern mythic themes such as virgin birth, divine child and slain god in the creation of a new and powerful story. So is it also a myth that archaeology and mythology are mismatched areas of scholarship?

It is certainly true that the intersection of the two fields of study raises a myriad of difficulties and questions – and for some it may be thought unworthy of any serious attention. After all the term 'myth' is often used in its modern negative sense as a falsehood or untrue report. We owe this usage to those Greek philosophers who claimed that rational discourse (*logos*) had supplanted the authoritative word or story (*mythos*) and to Christian writers who equated myth with the falsity of pagan belief. There are many well-known approaches to the study of myth including the psychoanalytical of Sigmund Freud and Carl Jung, the structuralist of Claude Lévi-Strauss, the sociological of Bronislaw Malinowski and the comparativist of Georges Dumézil, for example. As already mentioned, in an Irish context, it is the latter, the study of comparative mythology, that holds the promise of revealing something about past ideologies.

Archaeologists today may be forgiven for thinking that the pursuit of ancient myths lacks credibility and should be left to others of a more romantic disposition, perhaps agreeing with the eminent historian who wrote 'myths are not to be despised, but reading them literally is not to be recommended'.[13] Yet the belief that some may shed light on past beliefs or events is a persistent one, and of course it is this that encourages the quest for lost continents. There are those – in claiming that some myths contain historical facts and that the memory of actual events lie at their heart – who would argue that Hesiod's description of the battle between Zeus and the Titans (who are slain by the earth-shaking Zeus with a thunderbolt) was inspired by that same eruption of the volcano Thera on Santorini around 1650 BC.

Many archaeologists will be familiar with the image of the fire-breathing dragon guarding heathen gold in *Beowulf* and reasonably enough will simply consider this an expression of a belief that the contents a barrow may be guarded by supernatural forces. But following the line of thought that there may be some truth in such tales, it has been claimed that fire-breathing dragons who guard treasures in burial mounds, as in *Beowulf* for example, are supposed to be ultimately based on the notion that such graves may contain valuables and decomposed flesh creates flammable methane gas which, when it comes into contact with the flame of a grave-robber's torch, explodes. Combine this with the image of a resident lizard, snake or salamander and the basis of the myth is evident – or so it is claimed. The common belief in giants is similarly reinforced by the discovery and misinterpretation of large fossil bones – a mastodon or mammoth bone is about three times the size of a human femur.[14]

This approach to myth is not new. The eminent Victorian anthropologist Edward Burnett Tylor in his widely-read *Primitive Culture* saw myth as an aspect of primitive religion, a prescientific attempt to explain the physical world in a literal sense.[15] In Irish medieval legend, the absence of snakes in that island is credited to their banishment by Saint Patrick though today we know their absence is simply due to an impoverished post-glacial fauna. Tylor had another explanation, he believed their appearance in medieval legend was inspired by a knowledge of fossil ammonites with their curving snake-like shape and, according to him, such reptiles were devoid of any symbolic significance. A widespread belief in the essential historicity of some myths has prompted an enormous literature not just on Atlantis but on subjects such as the Biblical deluge and Noah's Ark – even though tales of primordial floods are widely diffused and to be found in almost every part of the world. Leonard Woolley (in his excavations at Ur in the 1920s) is but one of several eminent archaeologists who have claimed to have uncovered traces of the great flood.[16]

This sort of study of ancient myth is an entertaining diversion that deflects us from a consideration of the real significance of such stories. It could be argued that the Biblical story of Lazarus raised from the dead is ultimately based on the fact that some people thought to be dead are not and, to the surprise of the mourners, appear to come back to life. The myth of Lazarus is in fact a sacred tale of divine intervention in human affairs and fabulous beasts guarding burial mounds are an expression of a belief that burial mounds are portals to the Otherworld. Giants too are symbols of this alternative realm. Natural events are not explanations of myths, myths themselves *are* the explanation of these phenomena. In short, myth offers a basis for the comprehension of phenomena beyond ordinary experience and as exemplary myths they may illustrate important social principles and modes of behaviour.

This is not to say that surviving mythologies do not preserve some historical details because the written texts we now have are the product of a long process of adaptation and emendation of an older oral tradition. The end result may be sophisticated literary creations like the epic Cattle Raid of Cooley and the *Iliad* and *Odyssey* of Homer where questions of historicity will always be the subject of debate. It is the study of comparative mythology, however, that offers a surer route to the identification of ancient mythic themes that may reveal something unexpected about the past.

The mythology of ancient Greece is to be found, for the most part, in the works of Homer, Hesiod and the great tragedians but much older elements are to be found in inscriptions in Minoan Crete where offerings to divinities such as Zeus (Diwe) and Hera (Ere) are recorded. Roman mythology, greatly influenced by Greece, is preserved in the writings of Cicero, Virgil, Livy, Plutarch, Ovid and others, but older Indo-European elements have long been recognized therein. The myth of the sacred twins Romulus and Remus is just one example. We will encounter other mythical twins in Chapter 7.

There has, of course, been a long a fruitful relationship between archaeology and myth in the Classical world but elsewhere in western and northern Europe the situation is more complicated. But even here, in the study of Irish tradition in particular, it is evident that some mythic themes preserved in medieval texts – the remnants of former structures of much greater complexity – may have roots that are very old indeed. They may have been a part of belief systems of great antiquity in ancient Europe and beyond.

CHAPTER 3

Sacral Kingship – The Mythology

The importance of sacral kingship in prehistoric Ireland is not in doubt and the varied evidence has been explored in a number of important studies in recent decades.[1] Tara, in particular, is associated with kingship in myth and history but the modern visitor to Tara of the Kings – Teamhair na Rig – is probably nonplussed to find themselves on a hilltop dotted with grassy mounds and enclosures. Even though the modest hill has splendid views over the central plain of Ireland, its royal associations are not immediately apparent.

The old Irish name Temair is cognate with words like the Greek *temenos* meaning sacred enclosure and with the Latin *templum* or sacred precinct, its Indo-European root, **tem-*, meaning to cut.[2] The largest enclosure on the hill is Ráth na Rí (the Fort of the Kings) and the cutting of its great ditch inside an external bank demarcated just such a sacred space (Fig. 3.1). Various monuments occur within it and include Dumha na nGiall (the Mound of the Hostages), the Forrad (the King's Seat or inauguration mound) and Teach Cormaic (Cormac's House). The latter is an early medieval ringfort named after Cormac mac Airt, one of the most famous of Tara's kings, often portrayed as the ideal ruler. These names, like the others in use today, were first recorded in the 11th century and for the most part have mythological or historical connotations. To the south is a smaller enclosure called Ráth Laoghaire, named after an early medieval king of Tara.

Dumha na nGiall (the Mound of the Hostages) in the northern part of Ráth na Rí is a passage tomb dating to the 3rd millennium BC. Excavation has uncovered pre-tomb activity, including traces of a curving segment of ditch that is conceivably part of a late 4th millennium BC enclosure, indicating that Tara's story is thousands of

38   *Myth and Materiality*

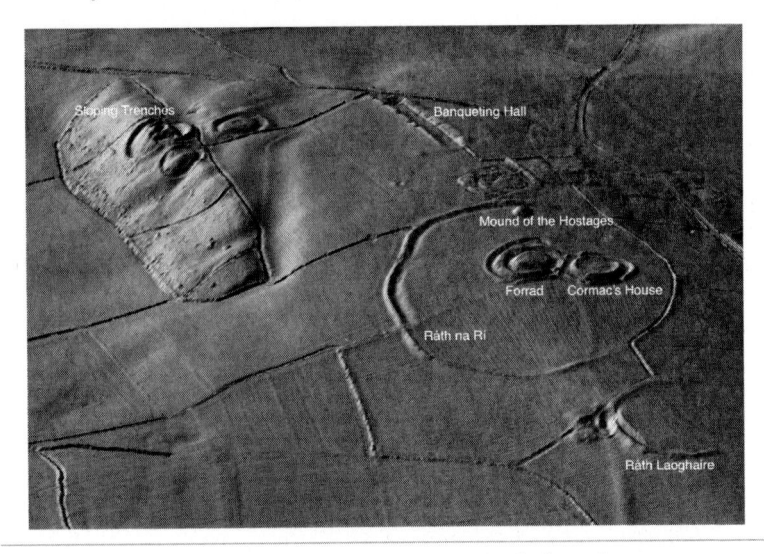

Figure 3.1. A LiDAR image of the Hill of Tara. This high resolution computer model of the summit of the hill clearly shows the large enclosure of Ráth na Rí in the centre-right of the picture with the Mound of the Hostages and the conjoined Forrad and Cormac's House within it. The ring barrows known as the Claoinfhearta (the 'Sloping Trenches') are on hill slope on the upper left. The parallel banks of the Banqueting Hall are visible in the upper centre. Ráth Laoghaire is on the lower right.

years old – for Bronze Age, Iron Age and early medieval activity is well attested on the hilltop too. There are numerous burial mounds to the north, many of them revealed by geophysical survey and the northern part of the hill in particular was once a great necropolis. Among these are several very large Iron Age ring barrows including a pair called the Claoinfhearta or 'the Sloping Trenches' situated on the western slopes of the hill. The northernmost was supposedly the dwelling of the king named Lugaid mac Con and is the subject of an especially interesting story in the 9th century *Cath Maige Mucrama* (The Battle of Mag Mucrama).[3]

This Lugaid mac Con was the predecessor of the celebrated Cormac mac Airt. The youthful Cormac, who was in fosterage there, was present when Lugaid delivered a judgement on a relatively minor matter of trespassing sheep. Some sheep had eaten the woad in the Queen's garden and the king ruled that the sheep should be surrendered as a penalty. Cormac demurred, saying that only the wool should be forfeit because the woad would grow again as would the wool. At first glance this is a charming story of a talented and precocious youth who will one day be king of Tara:

> Now on one occasion sheep ate the woad of Lugaid's queen. The matter was brought to Mac Con for decision. 'I pronounce', said Mac Con, 'that the sheep be forfeited for it'. Cormac, a little boy, was on the couch beside him. 'No, foster-father', said he, 'the shearing of the sheep for the cropping of the woad would be more just, for the woad will grow and the wool will grow on the sheep'. 'That is the true judgement', said all. 'Moreover, it is the son of the true prince who has given it'.

Lugaid mac Con's failure to see that the woad would grow again just like the wool on the sheep was a misjudgement with a catastrophic outcome:

> With that one side of the house falls down the cliff, namely the side in which the false judgement was given. It will remain for ever like that, the Claoinfhearta of Tara.

The collapse of the house proved to be the least of Lugaid's worries. For the account continues:

> After that he was a year in the kingship of Tara and no grass came through the earth, nor leaf on tree, nor grain in corn. So the men of Ireland expelled him from his kingship for he was an unlawful ruler.

This striking image of a land laid waste is one illustration of the calamitous results of a false judgement by a sacred king. It is an example of *fír flathemon*, the 'prince's truth', and it is just one of several indications that the institution of sacral kingship was a feature of prehistoric Ireland. The concept of the 'prince's truth' or 'the ruler's truth' is an integral element in the ideology of sacral kingship. It has

Myth and Materiality

been compared to the Hindu 'Act of Truth' (Sanskrit *satyā -kriyā*) for in both the Indian and Irish traditions there are tales in which the formal pronouncement of the truth is a magical act. The coincidences of idiom and episode suggest a common inheritance.[4] The just king guaranteed the order of the cosmos in the Indo-European world: in ancient India it is said in the *Rig Veda* 'By Truth, Mitra and Varuna, increasers of Truth, embracers of Truth, you have reached great insight', and in a Vedic hymn 'By Truth, the earth is supported, (and) the sky is supported, along with the sun.'[5]

The belief that truth was sacred is expressed in the early 8th century text *Audacht Morainn* (The Testament of Morann), the oldest *speculum principis*, or 'mirror of princes' in western Europe. Here a mythical judge addresses a mythical king at length and reminds him of the positive consequences of just rule: 'It is through the ruler's truth that he secures peace …'. As one scholar described it 'through *fír flathemon* comes prosperity and fertility for man, beast and crops; the seasons are temperate, the corn grows strong and heavy, mast and fruit are abundant on the trees, cattle give milk in plenty, rivers and estuaries teem with fish; plagues, famines and natural calamities are warded off; internal peace and victory over external enemies are guaranteed'.[6]

Other elements of the institution of sacral kingship are alluded to in other tales. Another king of Tara, Conaire Mór, had his kingship foretold in a vision that took place at a bull sacrifice reported in *Togail Bruidne Da Derga* (The Destruction of Da Derga's Hostel). Bull sacrifice may have been a part of the rituals of kingship too. The Conaire Mór rite took place at a *tairbfheis* or bull-feast in which a bull was killed, a man would eat its flesh and drink its broth and then lie down to sleep after an incantation was chanted over him; the person he would see in his sleep would be king:

> Then the king, namely Eterscél, died. A bull-feast (tairbfheis) was convened by the men of Ireland: that is, a bull used to be killed by them, and one man would eat his fill of it and drink its broth and a spell of truth was chanted over him in his bed. Whoever he would see in his sleep would be king; and the sleeper would perish if he uttered a falsehood.[7]

3. Sacral Kingship – The Mythology

There is also an account of a bull-feast held by Ailill and Medb to see who will be king of Tara in *Serglige Con Culainn* (The Wasting Sickness of Cú Chulainn):

> They made a bull-feast there then, so that they might learn from it to whom they should give the kingship. This is how the bull-feast used to be made: to kill a white bull, and for one man to eat his fill of its flesh and of its broth, and to sleep after that meal; and for four druids to chant a spell of truth over him. And the form of the man to be made king used to be shown to him in a dream, his shape and his description, and the manner of work that he was doing ....[8]

This account has been compared to the famous reference to druidic sacrifice in Pliny's *Historia Naturalis* and considered a part of the common Celtic inheritance of Gauls and Irish:

> Having made preparation for a ritual sacrifice and a banquet beneath a tree, they bring there two white bulls, whose horns are bound then for the first time. Clad in a white robe, a priest climbs a tree and cuts the mistletoe with a golden sickle, and it is caught in a white cloak. Then finally they kill the victim, praying that God will render this gift of his propitious to those to whom he has granted it.[9]

In the story The Destruction of Da Derga's Hostel, the term *bruiden*, translated as hostel, means a large hall or mansion and has no association with budget accommodation.[10] Much of this tale, written in the 10th or 11th century, is devoted to the tragic circumstances leading to the death of Conaire Mór but it also recounts his birth, the tests he has to pass and his elevation to kingship. When he is accepted as king in Tara, an Otherworldly figure enunciates the *geissi* or taboos placed on his reign. These are effectively contracts between a sacral king and the Otherworld:

> 'You shall not go righthandwise around Tara and lefthandwise around Brega. The evil beasts of Cerna must not be hunted by you. And you must not go out every ninth night beyond Tara. You must not sleep in a house from which firelight is visible

> after sunset and in which [light] is visible from outside. And three Reds shall not go before you into a Red's house. And no raiding shall be done in your reign. And after sunset a company of one woman or one man shall not enter the house in which you are. And you shall not settle the quarrel of your two slaves'.[11]

His reign was a prosperous golden age. There was 'such abundance of good will that no one slew any other in Ireland', there was plenty of fish in the rivers Bush and Boyne, there were no thunderstorms; in fact 'from mid-spring to mid-autumn no wind disturbed a cow's tail'. However, Conaire's foster brothers and their companions took to thieving and marauding and he failed to stop them thereby infringing one of the taboos, namely that there should be no raiding in his reign. He eventually took action, sparing his foster brothers but condemning their companions to death. Then, recognizing the unfairness of this decision, he revoked it and ordered all of them to be banished. With this injustice, he violated the 'prince's truth'.

This combination of breaking a taboo and delivering an unjust judgement appears to be an Irish instance of the Indo-European theme that Georges Dumézil called 'the single sin of the sovereign', namely an irreparable act that destroys the very *raison d'être* of sovereignty.[12] Observing one's taboos is being true to one's obligations. The doomed Conaire broke his other taboos one after the other, even failing to prevent three horsemen with red tunics, mantles, and weaponry and riding red horses (the three Reds who come from the Otherworld) from preceding him to Da Derga's hostel. Disaster follows and he and his followers die in its violent destruction.

Another central element in the ideology of sacral kingship is the sacred marriage (often called by the Greek term *hieros gamos*) between king and goddess. The Irish sacred marriage or *banais rígi* (from *ban+feis* 'woman-marriage', + *rígi* 'kingship') was a ritual mating in which a mythic sovereignty goddess granted the right to rule to a king who symbolically slept (*feis*) with her.

The wonders that mark the birth of the legendary Conn Cétchathach (Conn of the Hundred Battles) and the benefits his reign will bring are told in the 9th or 10th century text *Airne Fíngein* (Fíngein's Night-watch).

The wondrous events include the bursting of the Boyne from the well of Nechtan near Carbury Hill in Co. Kildare, the creation of the five great roads of Ireland, and the appearance of one of the great sacred trees of Ireland. The sacred tree is called the Éo Mugna, an oak that once stood in Co. Kildare (Chapter 6).

In *Baile in Scáil* (The Vision of the Spectre) Conn is transported to the Otherworld and granted foreknowledge of his future kingship and that of his successors in Tara. The sovereignty goddess appears as a beautiful woman seated beside the god Lug. He is described as a man of wondrous appearance seated on a throne, beside him the woman sits in a crystal chair and wears a golden diadem. Beside her is a silver vat, a golden ladle and a golden cup. The man declares he is no mere spectral apparition:

> My name is Lug, son of Ethliu, son of Tigernmas. For this reason I have come, to tell you the duration of your own rule, and that of every future ruler in Tara …

Lug's consort, the young woman, is described as the 'eternal Sovereignty of Ireland' and:

> It was she who gave this repast to Conn, an ox-rib and the rib of a boar. The ox-rib was twenty-four feet long, and there were eight feet between its flank and the ground. When the girl went to distribute the drink, she asked: 'To whom is this cup to be given?' The Spectre answered her. He named every ruler in turn from Conn's time until Doomsday ….[13]

Then all disappear but Conn retains the vat, the ladle and the cup. The offering of a drink by the goddess of sovereignty is, as we shall see, a highly symbolic act.

In *Echtra mac nEchach Muigmedóin* (The Adventure of the Sons of Eochaid Muigmedón) we are told how Níall Noígiallach (Niall of the Nine Hostages) wins the kingship of Tara in what is a piece of Uí Néill mythic propaganda.[14] He and his brothers were hunting and having consumed their prey seek to quench their thirst. One after another they come across a well that is guarded by a hideous female who demands a kiss in exchange for a drink of water. All except one of the brothers refuse. One does offer a kiss but Níall not only kisses her but also has intercourse with her:

> Niall went then to seek water, and reached the same well. 'Give me water, woman,' said he. 'Give me a kiss, and I will give it,' she answered. 'As well as giving you a kiss I will lie with you,' said he. Then he bent down over her and kissed her. Afterwards, however, when he looked at her, there was not in the world a girl fairer than her in appearance and form. Like the snowy residue in ditches was every bodily joint from head to sole. She had rounded queenly arms, graceful long fingers, straight, beautiful legs, and two rounded slippers of white bronze between her little soft-white feet and the ground. A costly purple mantle was around her, adorned with a bright silver brooch. She had shining pearly teeth, large queenly eyes, and lips red as rowan berries.
>
> 'You have many forms woman,' said the young man. 'True,' said she.
>
> 'Who are you?' asked the lad.
>
> 'I am Sovereignty,' said she.[15]

This is an instance in which the goddess has a loathsome aspect. The transformation of the ugly woman into a beautiful girl when she gains a fitting partner is a metaphorical reflection of the benefits that the land will gain from a lawful and just ruler. Rightful kingship will bring prosperity and success. Niall is ancestor of the Uí Néill dynasties and here myth is used to serve the purpose of projecting the Uí Néill claim to the sovereignty of Ireland back to mythical time. It is significant that the motif of offering a drink should figure in this tale too. The sovereignty figure Étaín who hailed from Ulster had a similar role. The serving of drink was her 'special gift' in the 9th century *Tochmarc Étaíne* (The Wooing of Étaín). When Eochaidh, king of Tara, had to choose a wife, he chose her from among fifty Otherworld women all of similar appearance declaring 'my wife is the best at serving drink in Ireland. I shall recognize her by her serving.'[16]

Medb Lethderg is the sovereignty goddess of Tara and her epithet Lethderg, red-sided or half-red, may be an allusion to the fact that the sovereignty of Ireland was half red or bloody, not just linked to land and fertility but also to martial violence. According to a genealogical miscellany in the Book of Lecan, she 'slept with nine kings of the kings of Ireland' and these included the father of Conn of the Hundred Battles, then his grandson Art, and later still Cormac mac Airt. It was said she 'would not allow a king in Tara without his having herself as a wife'. In short, she is depicted as the mate of a long succession of kings.

Another Medb is better known today. Medb of Crúachain, the great Queen Maeve of the *Táin*, also had a multiplicity of husbands and a name that linked her to the dispensing of mead as we have seen (Chapter 2). These links are another reflection of the importance of drinking ceremonial in the affirmation of kingship. There may be another allusion to this marriage rite in one version of the foundation myth of the Greek colony of Massalia (Marseille). Several writers have drawn attention to the account preserved by Aristotle of the wedding of Petta, daughter of the local king. The Greek Euxenus of Phocaea was an invited guest and the bride, instead of offering a bowl of wine to whoever was to marry her, gave it to Euxenus. Her father believed she had acted according to the will of the gods and Euxenus took her as his wife. He founded the colony and their descendants lived in Massalia thereafter. It is true that not every cup-bearing woman is necessarily a goddess of sovereignty but the Celtic name of the bride Petta is probably important in this context, as *pett* or *pitt* may mean a holding of land. In recording this story, Aristotle in the 4th century BC may have inadvertently recorded an early Celtic myth.[17]

This sort of sovereignty figure appears again in Paeonia, modern Macedonia, in a story recorded by Herodotus in the 5th century BC. In his *Histories*, he tells the tale of two Paeonian brothers Pigres and Mantyes who offered their sister to the great Persian king Darius I:

> So when Darius crossed into Asia, these men came to Sardis, and brought with them their sister, who was a tall and beautiful woman. Then waiting till Darius sat in state in the capital city of the Lydians they had their sister dressed in the richest gear they could and sent her to draw water, bearing a jar on her head, and leading a horse by the bridle on her arm, while

all the way as she went she span flax. Now as she passed by Darius, he took notice of her; for what she did was not in the manner of Persians or the Lydians or any of the peoples of Asia. Darius accordingly noted her, and ordered some of his guard to follow her and watch to see what she would do with the horse. So they followed her: and the woman, when she came to the river, first watered the horse, then filled her vessel and came back the same way, with the jar of water on her head, leading the horse on her arm, while she still kept twirling the spindle.

Marvelling at what he heard from his watchers and what he saw for himself, Darius bade the woman be brought before him. When she had been brought, her brothers, who watched all this from a place nearby, came too. Darius asked of what nation she was, and the young man told him that they were Paeonians and that she was their sister. 'But who', he answered, 'are the Paeonians, and where do they dwell, and with what intent have you come to Sardis?' They told him, that they had come to be his men, that the towns of Paeonia lay on the Strymon, a river not far from the Hellespont, and that they were colonists from the Teucrians of Troy. So they told him all this, and the king asked them if all the women of their country were so industrious. To this too they very readily answered (for it was for this very purpose that they had come), that it was indeed so.

What happened to the woman, we are not told, but Darius ordered all Paeonians, men, women and children, to be brought to him.

The ritualized actions of the woman are noteworthy. She is also richly dressed and her attributes include a vessel containing water, a horse and a spindle. Elements recall the story of Euxenus and Petta and that of Niall of the Nine Hostages, and the close association of horses and sovereignty is reflected here as well. This woman is the personification of sovereignty and Darius is, in effect, being offered the kingship of Paeonia in this story.[18]

A much later allusion to the sovereignty concept combined with the world tree and *axis mundi* is to be found in the Breton legend of St Judicael. The tale of the warrior-saint Judicael who reigned in the

3. Sacral Kingship – The Mythology

7th century was probably composed in the early 11th century but is derived in part from an Old Breton original. It narrates the youthful vision of Judicael's father Iudael and begins:

> One night, Iud-hael, most noble king, then yet of but youthful years, weary after hunting, slept in the house of his subject Ausoc, in Trefles, which is at the end of the long coastline on the west, within the limits of Bra Leon and Kemenet Ili. In a dream he saw a most lofty mountain standing in the middle of his kingdom, *i.e.* in its very centre. It was difficult to reach by way of a stony track. And there, at the summit of that mountain, he saw himself seated in an ivory chair. And within his view there was a wondrous huge post in the form of a round column, founded by its roots in the ground, its mighty branches reaching the sky, and its straight shaft reaching from the earth up to the heavens …
>
> And just then, he saw next to him the daughter of his subject Ausoc. She was named Pritell, a lovely girl, as yet unknown by man, whom he had seen the previous day and had desired in his mind. Immediately, she saluted him in the manner of a subordinate, saying, 'Hail, lord Iud-hael!' Then, turning to look at her, he said, 'Girl, what are you doing here?' She answered him: 'My king Iud-hael, in some manner it has been fore-ordained by our maker that you and I should come to this place, and that the custody of this ornamental pillar should be handed on for a time from no man in the world but yourself to no woman but myself and that after that it be passed on from no woman other than myself to no man but yourself' ....

Iudael dreams that he was seated on an ivory chair on the summit of a mountain in the middle of his kingdom in north-western Brittany. Nearby a great tree, its roots in the ground and its branches in the heavens, richly decorated with weaponry, spurs, bridles and saddles, gold and candles, stretched from the earth to the heavens. A beautiful virgin named Pritell appears whose physical union with him brings prosperity to him and his kingdom and produces a child who will become the saint. This is an echo of the theme of sacred marriage between king and goddess placed significantly at the sacred centre of the kingdom.[19]

The presence of a horse in the Paeonian story – and perhaps the horse equipment in Iudael's vision – are both reflections of an important Indo-European element in the rituals of sacred marriage. Equine rituals and horse sacrifice may have been important features, and again the Irish evidence for the latter is often cited. The Welsh clergyman Giraldus Cambrensis writing in the 12th century, and ever anxious to depict the Irish as less than civilized, recorded a valuable piece of antiquarian lore from remote Donegal. This was the inauguration rite of the Cenél Conaill, a northern branch of the Uí Néill:

> When the whole people of that land has been gathered together in one place, a white mare is brought forward into the middle of the assembly. He who is to be inaugurated, not as a chief, but as a beast, not as a king, but as an outlaw, embraces the animal before all, professing himself to be a beast also. The mare is then killed immediately, cut up in pieces, and boiled in water. A bath is prepared for the man afterwards in the same water. He sits in the bath surrounded by all his people, and all, he and they, eat of the meat of the mare which is brought to them. He quaffs and drinks of the broth in which he is bathed, not in any cup, or using his hand, but just dipping his mouth into it about him. When this unrighteous rite has been carried out, his kingship and dominion has been conferred.[20]

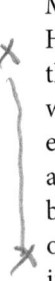

Many writers have pointed out that this rite has parallels with the Hindu *asva-medha* or horse sacrifice in which the principal spouse of the king submits to a symbolic union with a dead stallion. The animal was suffocated – no blood being shed. In ancient India – at the other end of the Indo-European world – the ritual involved a stallion and a woman while the Irish ceremony concerned a king and a mare but both included a symbolic union and the killing and dismemberment of a horse to ensure fertility and prosperity and both rites culminated in the consumption of parts of the animal.[21]

Horse sacrifice was known in ancient Rome and several contemporary writers refer to it. The killing was known as the *October Equus – the October Horse*. A stallion, that had won a chariot race and was the right-hand animal in a chariot pair, was dedicated to Mars and killed with a spear thrust. The horse was then partly dismembered: its tail and head were removed. There was a contest for the head and the bleeding tail was carried to an altar in the building known as the Regia where there was a shrine to Mars. Even though the element of a symbolic mating is absent, this unique Roman event has been seen as an another echo of the Indo-European rite.[22]

There may be echoes of equine rites in a sovereignty figure's links with horses. This is particularly evident in some of the mythology associated with Macha of Emain Macha or Navan Fort (Chapter 7). However, the multiple liaisons, already mentioned, of Medb Lethderg of Tara and Medb of Crúachain are perhaps the clearest echoes of this symbolic marriage. Ailill was king of Connacht because of his marriage to Medb and her several matings are a reflection of her role as sovereignty figure with whom the reign of each pagan king was inaugurated in a mystic union. Such numerous pairings have Mesopotamian parallels too where the sacred marriage between king and goddess is documented as early as the 3rd millennium BC.[23]

To return to Tara – there are significant links between kingship and chariotry where again horses play an important role. Embracing an ugly goddess of sovereignty was not the only mythic ordeal a prospective king might face. There may have been other challenges, ones even involving a symbolic chariot race and untamed horses. The tests faced by the king Conaire Mór are recounted in *De Shíl Chonairi Móir* (Of the Seed of Conaire Mór):

> There was a king's chariot at Tara. To the chariot were yoked two steeds of the same colour, which had never before been harnessed. It would tilt up before any man who was not destined to receive the kingship of Tara, so that he could not control it, and the horses would spring at him. And there was a king's mantle in the chariot; whoso might not receive Tara's sovereignty the mantle was ever too big for him. And there

were two flag-stones in Tara: 'Blocc' and 'Bluigne'; when they accepted a man, they would open before him until the chariot went through. And Fál was there, the 'stone penis' at the head of the chariot course; when a man should have the kingship of Tara, it screeched against his chariot axle, so that all might hear. But the two stones Blocc and Bluigne would not open before one who should not hold the sovereignty of Tara, and their usual position was such, that one's hand could not pass sideways between them; also he who was not to hold Tara's kingship, the Fál would not screech against his axle. They had not received Lugaid Ríabnderg, once Eterscél had been slain.[24]

While the aforementioned Lugaid Ríabnderg clearly failed his test, Conaire is successful – with some support from the Otherworldly hosts of the *síd* summoned by his supernatural mother. He enters Tara to be acclaimed by the oracular stone of Fál:

The chariot and its steeds awaited him with the cloak of kingship in the chariot. The steeds stayed behind there for Conaire. 'Lo! a chariot for thee,' said his mother. Conaire enters the chariot, and it receives him. 'Gird the cloak about thee', said she. He dons it standing in presence of the hosts: the cloak fitted him. He stands in the chariot and it moves under him. He goes towards the two stones and they open before him. He goes to the Fál with all the host around him and his mother before him. The Fál cries out. 'Fál has accepted him!' cry the hosts. The hosts in Tara decline to give them battle; and make submission to Conaire and render to him his father's heritage. They acknowledge him as son of Eterscél Mór and give him the sovereignty and his father's territories; he makes seizures (of lands) for his hosts and till the ninth day from then he provides for them. They leave a bidding with him: that the sun should neither set nor rise on him in Tara.

Physical perfection was another essential quality of a sacral king in Irish tradition. The most famous example is the mythical Nuadu of the Tuatha Dé Danann who lost an arm and was provided with a silver replacement so he could remain king, hence his epithet *Argatlám* 'silver hand'. Otherwise this blemish would have disqualified him from the kingship. The only king cited in the medieval laws as losing the kingship of Tara is the 7th century Congal Cáech who was blinded in one eye by a bee. The death of the renowned Cormac mac Airt was preceded by his exile a year before to Achaill, the hill of Skreen to the east of Tara, because he lost an eye in a confrontation.

A memory of the significance of royal mutilation also survives in elements of the legend of the Breton saint Melor. His father, the king, brought great prosperity to the land but was killed by Melor's uncle Rivod who proceeded to mutilate him by cutting off Melor's right hand and left foot to debar him from the kingship. Rivod's unjust reign was disastrous and Melor was miraculously given a silver hand and a bronze foot by an angel. Despite all these tribulations he was eventually decapitated but posthumously became a noted wonder-working saint.[25]

It is generally thought that traditional kingship in Gaul had declined by the time of Julius Caesar who has little to say on the matter. However, over a century later when Tacitus mocked Mariccus of the Boii for pretending to be divine and calling himself a god, he may unwittingly have recorded an important detail:

> I am ashamed to say that a certain Mariccus, a commoner of the tribe of the Boii, boldly endeavoured to thrust himself into greatness and to challenge the armies of Rome, pretending to be divine. This champion of Gaul, and god, as he had entitled himself, had already gathered a force of 8,000 men, and was beginning to influence the neighbouring Aeduan cantons. But the chief community of the Aedui wisely sent out a picked force, and Vitellius provided auxiliaries in support; they scattered the mob of fanatics. Mariccus was captured in the engagement, and later thrown to wild beasts. As they refused to devour him, the common people stupidly believed him invulnerable, until he was executed in the presence of Vitellius.[26]

Elements of a belief in sacral kingship in Continental Europe may have survived the Roman conquest for it is quite possible the desperate Mariccus, at a time of great crisis, was deliberately invoking the old order to encourage his followers in their challenge to the power of Rome.

Briefly, a central theme of Irish sacral kingship is the concept that the king was wedded in a symbolic marriage to a supernatural woman who personified his kingdom. The ritual may have involved a ceremonial offering of drink, horse sacrifice, bull sacrifice and ritualistic chariotry. The sacral king is identified with the land and the cosmos, and is a mediator between this world and the Otherworld. The maintenance of the cosmic order and the prosperity of the land were dependent on a just ruler who was an unblemished individual who observed his contractual obligations with the Otherworld – namely each *geis* or taboo imposed on him. Archaeological props in the sacral theatre may have included ancestral burial mounds, pillar stones, timber pillars, ceremonial enclosures both large and small, and processional ways.

It is interesting that elements of the institution of sacral kingship should be detectable not only in Ireland but also in very different though shadowy guises as far afield as Brittany, southern France and south-eastern Europe. It has been argued that the linguistic evidence would suggest that all Indo-European peoples were, at one time or another, probably ruled by tribal kings. Indo-European *$r\bar{e}g$-s*, the ancestor of Sanskrit *rāj-*, Latin *rēx* and Irish *rí*, with Welsh *rhi* and Gaulish *-rīx*, all point to this. Some of these tribal leaders – who achieved particular power and prominence – may have been sacral kings. Size may not have mattered, of course, as ethnographic analogies remind us. Among the Rukuba of Nigeria, for example, the term king might be applied to the ruler of a village of 50 people or to one who ruled 2000. A Rukuba king had few taboos though he was forbidden to have contact with or eat certain types of leaves and may be deposed if his mystical power failed to protect his people from any kind of catastrophe.[27]

The sacred king is a widespread phenomenon around the world and has been the subject of an enormous body of literature since the time of James Frazer's 19th century *The Golden Bough*, famously inspired by the tale of the *rex Nemorensis*, who in a sacred grove dedicated to Diana at Nemi in southern Italy, had to murder his predecessor and was murdered in turn – in Macauley's memorable words: 'The priest who slew the slayer, and shall himself be slain'. As Frazer showed a large body of ethnographical and historical evidence demonstrates that this is a kingly institution that is not primarily political, that to reign does not mean to govern[28] but to guarantee the order of the world and society. There are many different models recorded in literary and anthropological studies. In Mesopotamia and elsewhere we encounter the deification of kings where the goddess in the form of a priestess chooses a ruler to act as her bridegroom. It is necessary to clearly distinguish between a king who is considered to be a god and one, in an Irish context, that is a sacred figure of unblemished physique, bound by ritual prescriptions and invested with quasi-divine qualities in that sacred marriage. The Irish prescription that required the deposition of a physically imperfect king differs only in degree from Frazer's belief that a divine king must die or be killed to ensure the order and fertility of the earth. However his assertion that one of the functions of a sacred king was that of rain-maker is clearly superfluous in an Irish context.[29]

Although there is a general consensus that sacral kingship was an institution in pre-Christian Ireland, the evidence elsewhere in Europe is tenuous, as we have seen in the case of the sovereignty figure. More often than not, the matter is the subject of much scholarly dispute. This has been the case in Scandinavia where the sacral character of its pagan rulers has been debated for many years. It has been suggested that the incestuous relationship between the god Freyr, associated with fertility, with his sister Freya, a goddess of war noted for her numerous sexual liaisons, is an echo of some form of sacred marriage. The same has been claimed for the relationship between Odin and his mistress Jord, the personification of the earth whose name is sometimes a poetic term for the land.

The story of the sacrifice of the king Dómaldi is recounted in several texts. His rule was marked by famine and this prompted his people to hold a great ritual sacrifice (*blót*) each autumn. At first they sacrificed oxen but famine persisted. Then they held human sacrifice but this too was not successful. It was finally agreed that the king had to be sacrificed. Evidently it was believed that the misfortunate Dómaldi had failed in his sacred duty to safeguard the fertility of the land.[30] Instances of kings performing ritual sacrifices are recorded as well, sometimes to greet the summer or the winter, and this, it has been suggested, indicates that 'the royal *blót* shows us the king as the creator of a new year and as the link between time and eternity'.[31] The claim that elements of sacral kingship may be traced in Germanic and Anglo-Saxon kingship is debated too. It rests on slender details such as the divine descent of the king from Odin and the king's sacral 'luck' or right relationship with the divine.[32]

In ancient Rome, the *Rex Sacrorum* inherited some of the powers of Roman kingship. With the foundation of the Republic and the abolition of kingship in the 6th century BC, this individual became the principal and most prestigious member of the priestly class. According to legend, the former powers of the king were divided, two consuls acted as military commanders while the *Rex Sacrorum* continued to perform the king's sacral function in the early republic.[33] He had no political role but did perform sacrifices at prescribed times but other than the continued use of the term 'king' and of sacrificial practice, there are few clues as to the nature and duties of the earlier kingship.

At an earlier date, at the eastern end of the Mediterranean, there are intriguing references to a conspicuous figure of exalted status in the tablets from various Mycenaean palaces inscribed in Linear B – that early form of Greek. Linear B texts found at palaces such as Pylos and Mycenae indicate that a person called a *wanax* was of the highest importance. In later Greek the term is used almost exclusively as an epithet of divinities while *basileus* is the common word for king. In the Linear B texts the *wanax* is clearly at the summit of the social hierarchy and had religious duties and powers. The very limited nature of the information in these sources is acknowledged. Many aspects of the role of the *wanax* are unknown and the meaning of the name is uncertain. Even so there are references that associate him or people linked to him with religious lands and he is recorded as presiding over or undergoing some form of initiation. In one text a person named Ekhelawon was the principal contributor to a sacrifice in the Pylos area and it is suggested he may have been a *wanax*. He contributes a bull to a sacrifice to Poseidon. If so this individual is the only named *wanax* known. Only the elite *wanax* and Poseidon are entitled to offerings of perfumed oil.[34] The *wanax* has generally been considered the king of a palace and its palatial territory and it does seem as if there was a sacral dimension to his office.

CHAPTER 4

Kings in Archaeology

It is very evident that most archaeologists prefer not to use the term 'king' when attempting to interpret the elite elements of society in prehistoric Europe. This is probably because there is an understandable association of kingship with state formation and with absolute monarchy. Well might a poet ask: Where are now the warring kings?[1]

Various sorts of elites have been claimed to have existed in the past. Inspired by ethnographic analogies, chiefdoms emerged as a popular interpretation in the 1970s to explain the complexity of the archaeological record in the Bronze Age and earlier Iron Age in particular. Terms such as chief and chiefdom are commonly preferred and chiefdoms have proved to be a resilient though debated concept. Kings are rarely acknowledged and it is interesting to note that the title 'chief' was promoted by British Colonial administrators from the early 19th century onwards in their African colonies as a substitute for the term 'king' since only the British monarch might bear that title.[2]

The Irish literary evidence for the institution of sacral kingship and the fragmentary indications found elsewhere should at least alert archaeologists to the distinct possibility that some of the elites identified in the prehistoric archaeological record had a sacral character.

The literary clues provided by Queen Medb would indicate that in all probability Rathcroghan was the inauguration place of sacral kings in pagan times. It is therefore reasonable to ask where is the archaeological evidence for a late prehistoric elite of any description in the general area? At first glance it is disconcerting to note that there are no hillforts or wealthy settlements or rich burials known from this part of Roscommon at this time – but there are some other clues.

4. Kings in Archaeology

A bronze cauldron recorded from Derreen townland, near Castlerea, just over 10 km south-west of Rathcroghan is a significant find. Probably dating to around 1200 BC, it is an early example of a vessel type well known in Atlantic Europe: similar pieces come from southern England and western France. The patrons who commissioned them must have been people of considerable power and status and it is generally believed these were ceremonial vessels that served as centre pieces at communal feasts. Their use may have been highly ritualized and much later in time cauldrons certainly have a magical character in medieval Welsh and Irish literature. In Homeric Greece they were a part of the prestigious belongings of Bronze Age kings and heroes. In the *Odyssey* they were a part of the precious possessions of Odysseus for instance and it is clear in the *Iliad* that the gift of a cauldron was mark of high esteem.[3]

Another notable item comes from the site of a former lake in Loughnaneane townland, near Roscommon town some 20 km to the south. If this is the Connacht lake mentioned in an early tale as Loch na nÉn, 'the lake of the birds', then it has noteworthy Otherworldly associations. It has been described as the entryway to a supernatural place where you will find fine plaintive fairy music and be able to drink mead from bright vessels along with other delights (Chapter 5). Discovered around 1840, this unique object essentially consists of two broad bands composed of multiple chains of linked bronze rings forming an oval piece with each end connected by a large circular ring containing a wheel-shaped design. Its present maximum length is about 90 cm (Fig. 4.1). Though incomplete, its slightly arched rectangular central pieces suggest that it may have been an insignia of high rank worn around the neck and over both shoulders as a sort of broad decorative collarette or tabard, the ends hanging down the back and down the chest. All elements are of cast bronze, the chains consisting of conjoined links each composed of three rings.

The closest parallels for this sort of chain-link construction are to be found among late Bronze Age chain-link objects of different forms in central Europe.[4] Objects like this may have been a part of the decorative gear of a warrior. While the manufacturing technique finds

58   *Myth and Materiality*

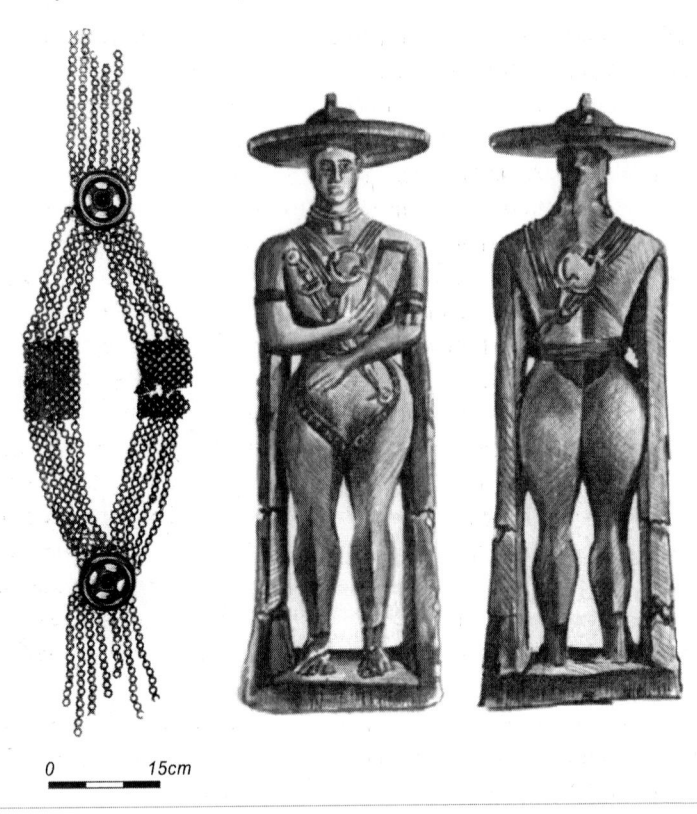

Figure 4.1. Left. Bronze cardiophylax from Loughnaneane, Co. Roscommon. Right. Larger than life-size stone statue of an armed warrior from Capestrano with cardiophylax on chest and back (no scale).

parallels in central Europe, there are parallels of another sort further west. A series of three-dimensional late Bronze Age carvings in northwestern Iberia schematically depict armed figures wearing emblematic devices on their chest or on their back. These designs are usually of slender sub-rectangular form and their meaning is debated. However they are generally accepted as symbols of authority and power and have been variously interpreted as an element of ceremonial dress, a representation of an ox- or bull-hide, or a cardiophylax or breastplate.[5] In fact, the Loughnaneane object is probably a form of cardiophylax (literally 'heart protector'), a symbolic protective device that may take the form of a pair of metal discs worn respectively on the chest and back of a warrior. It is well known in south-eastern France and the Iberian peninsula from the 7th to the 4th centuries BC, and in the Greek and Roman world. A good example occurs on the famous Capestrano statue from eastern Italy dated to the 6th century BC.[6]

This Roscommon find is an exceptional discovery so far west. It must fall into a category of exotic material of Continental origin to be associated with prestigious royal sites and – so far at least – a type not recorded in Britain at this date. The remains of the Barbary Ape found in Navan Fort is another example of this sort of exotica. So too is the Tamlaght hoard of bronze objects found less than two kilometres west of Navan. It comprised a sword of native type, a bronze ring, a decorated cup of Jenišovice type and a Fuchsstadt bowl.[7] These vessels, presumably related to drinking ceremonial, are well represented in Central Europe where they are dated to approximately 1000 BC. Objects like these, whether of Bronze Age or Iron Age date, demonstrate a capacity to access networks of long-distance exchange and a preoccupation with the acquisition of exceptional marks of social distinction.

Another unique status symbol comes from northern Roscommon and it too is an old and poorly recorded find. It was found in a field at Tumna, north-west of Carrick-on-Shannon, in 1840, about 20 km to the north-east of Rathcroghan. It comprised eleven (or perhaps thirteen) large golden beads. Each bead was a hollow ball fashioned from two hemispheres of thin sheet gold fused together and perforated to allow them to be strung together (Fig. 4.2). Of different sizes (from 9.7 cm to 6.8 cm in diameter – the size of a lemon) they seem to have comprised a splendid and ostentatious neck ornament of graduated beads. It has been calculated that an original necklace of thirteen beads would have weighed in or around 772 grams; this is a significant amount of gold being the equivalent of at least three gold collars or gorgets. It seems very likely they represent an attempt to replicate in gold large amber beads of similar size and shape.[8]

A quite outstanding discovery was made in 1861 in the course of turf cutting in Ardnaglug bog in Knock townland, Co. Roscommon,

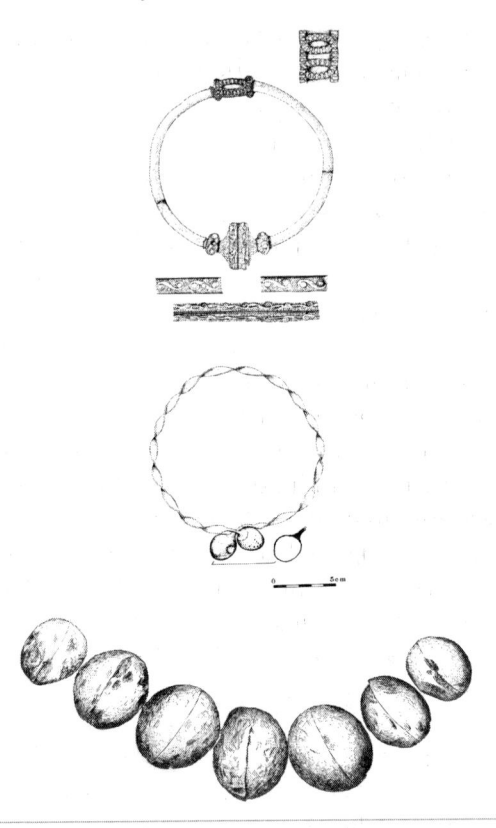

Figure 4.2. Above. Gold torcs from Knock, Co. Roscommon. Below. Some of the gold beads from Tumna, Co. Roscommon (no scale).

about 40 km to the south. Two gold torcs or neck rings were found in a wooden box (that was not preserved) and for many years they were erroneously believed to have been found near Clonmacnoise.[9] The objects are torcs of quite different type, one is a buffer torc, the other a ribbon torc (Fig. 4.2). The latter is a loosely twisted and simple neck ornament. It has unusual hollow pear-shaped terminals that may represent acorns and carry some symbolic meaning. Another ribbon torc made from a band of loosely spiral twisted gold and now in the British Museum was found near Ballinameen south of Boyle in the

19th century. It has simple hooked terminals and belongs to a type that probably dates to an earlier period *c.* 1400 BC. Thus these simple but prestigious ornaments may have has a much longer pedigree in this part of the world.

The buffer torc is a celebrated and much discussed piece belonging a well-known British and Continental type of penannular neck ring with broad, flat, expanded, circular terminals or 'buffers'. The Knock example is a version where the terminals have been joined together to form a single element. It basically consists of two semicircular hollow tubes of sheet gold that fit into hollow decorative expansions at front and back. At the front (and worn beneath the chin), the conjoined buffers are flanked by bosses, one of which is perforated to take a pin which secured one detachable tubular section of the torc. At the back, a rectangular element is decorated with pronounced convex mouldings which form in part a pair of interlocking oval loops ornamented with a sinuous pattern of applied gold wire. The elegant La Tène decoration on the flanking bosses of the biconical element at the front consists of pairs of repoussé S-scrolls, that on the central part consists of two narrow panels of irregular, asymmetrical, sinuous tendrils with spiral bosses. The background is finely stippled to accentuate the ornament.

This type of torc and the repoussé decoration, in particular the asymmetrical tendril motif, find general parallels on the Continent in the early La Tène period and, if not an import as sometimes suggested, it was made by someone familiar with torcs and other fine metalwork in the Rhineland around or shortly after 300 BC.[10] It thus represents the earliest evidence for contact with or emulation of exponents of La Tène or Celtic art. This remarkable art style developed in eastern France and western Germany, in the region of the Marne and the Rhine, in the 5th century BC and is found mainly on fine metalwork in rich aristocratic burials. Many of the motifs, like the tendril, are derived from Classical plant motifs, sometimes transformed almost beyond recognition.

Among other important finds discovered within a radius of 40 km or less from Rathcroghan are a major hoard that included bronze rings, penannular rings covered with gold leaf, amber beads and boar's tusks found in Rathtinaun on the shores of Lough Gara and a very large gold 'dress-fastener' weighing over 16 oz (450+ grams) found at Castlekelly, Co. Galway. Some two dozen bronze swords have been recorded in the county and two bronze shields from the River Shannon are all testimony to the presence of a warrior caste who probably favoured sword and spear. One shield is a small sheet bronze buckler simply decorated with four bosses, the other is a superb and ornate specimen found in the river near Barrybeg, north of Athlone. Decorated with multiple concentric ribs and bosses, and just over 66 cm in diameter with a thickness of just 9 mm, this is a piece of armour made primarily for display. It is also a shield type well represented in Britain.[11]

The identification of sacral kings in the archaeological record is not an easy task even when rich burials and elaborate settlement evidence are present – but these objects are all testimony to the exceptional importance of this part of Roscommon in late prehistoric times. It is worth noting this area was important in the earlier Bronze Age as well. A large circular mound at Grange, just south of Rathcroghan, contained the unburnt and cremated remains of some twenty-five people, several accompanied by finely-made pottery vessels of the Bowl Tradition. One secondary cremation in an urn of the Vase Tradition was the burial of a young adult male accompanied by a bronze dagger that had been deliberately and ritually destroyed by folding it over several times and burning it on the cremation pyre. Judging from the half dozen radiocarbon dates available it is possible that the burial activity at Grange was quite protracted and may have spanned a period of about 400 years. The dagger, dated to around 1700 BC, has a flat grooved blade and six rivets, a type with parallels in prestigious burials in southern England and, indeed, related to an example from the well-known Bush Barrow (Fig. 4.6, 4). One fascinating later find is some iron slag, a furnace bottom and a deep deposit of charcoal discovered on the northern edge of the mound. Though undated, it seems likely that an Iron Age or even an early medieval iron smith deliberately chose this location to undertake a task that had magical associations. The ancient burial mound may have been perceived as a charmed place that gave added significance to the iron produced there.[12]

4. Kings in Archaeology

Elsewhere in the funerary sphere, terms such as princely grave, *tombe princière* or *Fürstengrab* are commonly used on the Continent in the Hallstatt and early La Tène Iron Age for burials marked by elaborate grave construction and particular grave goods. Some of these special individuals could well have had royal status but identifying a sacral dimension is obviously a real challenge. As Conor Newman has indicated, writing of Tara, context is important: 'key elements of the mythology and rituals of sacral kingship are, by their very nature, beyond the range of scientific detection. Archaeologists should be alert, however, to the fact that in highly charged religious contexts such as this, even the mundane is potentially pregnant with magico-religious significance: how else, indeed, would the routines and objects of everyday life be brought into the benign orbit of religion?'[13]

Of course, exceptional burials – especially those that part significantly from any norm – may be a promising area of study. Parker Pearson has drawn attention to some Yorkshire chariot burials with unusual grave goods that do seem to be the graves of dominant if not royal groups. Some display 'rites of reversal' as with the coat of iron chain-mail placed on the body in a chariot burial at Kirkburn that had been laid upside-down and back to front (Fig. 5.2). This sort of reversal (or inversion) may be an allusion to the Otherworld (Chapter 5), an ever present concern in the life of a sacred king as we have seen. Interestingly, this burial of an adult male contained the bronze mounts of the D-shaped lid of some kind of organic container but no weaponry.[14]

The high status of such cart or chariot burials is not in doubt and, remembering the association of chariotry and kingship at Tara, it seems entirely reasonable to consider such male graves as kingly burials. There may have been a particular symbolism in the dismantling of the chariot (and presumably in the act of leading the horses away). Dismantling could of course simply represent the decommissioning of the vehicle akin to the ritual neutralizing of a weapon. It is worth noting, however, that this was not the case in an earlier chariot burial found at Newbridge near Edinburgh probably dating to about 400 BC. The chariot here had been buried intact in a large pit with slots dug to take the wheels at one end of the grave and the yoke, other fitments and bridle bits placed at the other. The human remains did not survive and there were no grave goods.[15] The symbolism here was of a different order and a likely indication that the process of dismantling probably does have some special significance and was not just an attempt to fit a large object into a small space. In Homeric epic, the combination of horse and chariot symbolizes power, life and consciousness, and their decoupling may have been a metaphor for the departure of the soul or spirit from the body at death.[16]

Inverted objects with Otherworldly connotations also occur in a rich and unusual burial at Mill Hill in Kent. The grave was found near the summit of a ridge overlooking the sea on the outskirts of Deal. A simple pit contained the extended skeleton of a 30–35 year old man with his left arm lying slightly bent across his pelvis (Fig. 4.3). His shield, represented by its bronze fitments and decorated plaque on the boss, covered the left side of the body. An iron sword in a decorated bronze scabbard rested on his right arm and the scabbard had been placed face down, in an inverted position. There was a decorated bronze suspension ring nearby, also placed face down. A decorated bronze brooch (that may have once been attached to an inverted cloak) lay on the left shin. A crown was found on the skull and comprised a decorated bronze band that was worn around the head with a plain bronze strip that covered the top of the head. The engraved decoration on the band is a slender symmetrical wave design with, at its centre, a rosette- or wheel-like motif that could be construed as a solar symbol.

Interestingly, various items in the grave appeared to have been old when buried and seemed to have had disparate life histories. The crown showed signs of wear and the sword did not fit well into the scabbard for instance. This means that rather than being the personal possessions of the individual, they might represent an assemblage designed to create an image of a warrior for someone who had some other special significance.[17]

The wider context is interesting too. This burial lay about 40 m north-west of the site of a large Bronze Age barrow that must once have been a very prominent monument. It became the focus for at least two cemeteries of Iron Age burials and a later extensive series

4. *Kings in Archaeology* 65

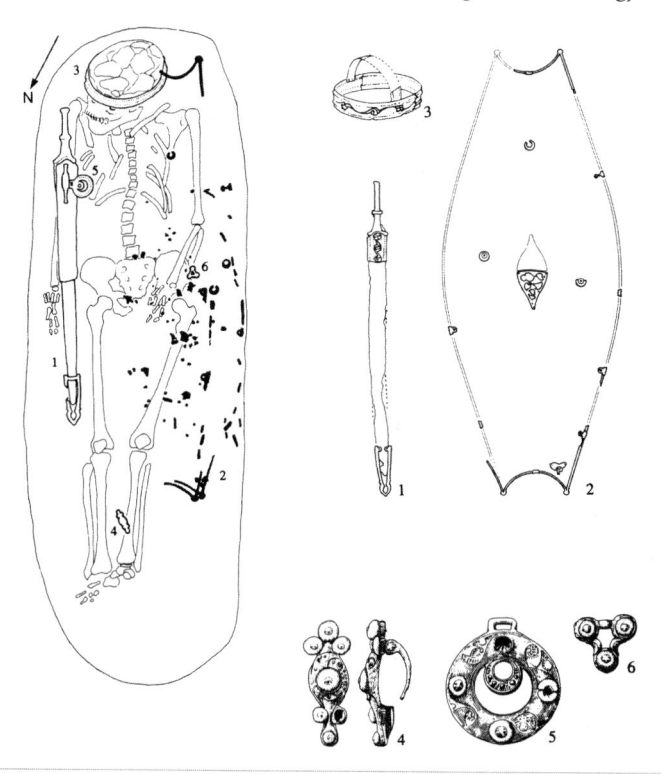

Figure 4.3. A male burial at Mill Hill, Deal, Kent, was accompanied by an inverted iron sword, a shield and a bronze brooch. A bronze crown was found on the skull with engraved decoration that comprised a wave design with, at its centre, a rosette- or wheel-like motif perhaps a solar symbol.

of Anglo-Saxon graves. The Iron Age burials were mostly simple elongated pits containing unburnt skeletons; only a few had grave goods such as brooches of the mid-2nd to mid-1st centuries BC. The largest burial group, the south-west cemetery, also contained a horse burial, the complete skeleton of a six to seven year old mare. The nearest grave held the remains of a young adult male and, not unreasonably, it was suggested this may have been the burial of a horse and rider. Both these were about 50 m south of the burial with the crown but, of course, there may be no connection between the two.

An unusual find was the discovery of a subterranean shrine 30 m south-east of the barrow site. This consisted of a 2.5 m deep chalk-cut vertical shaft leading to an underground chamber that, judging from Roman pottery sherds, had been filled in some time in the 2nd century AD. A small chalk carving of a human figure found in the fill may once have stood in a niche in the north-western chamber wall. The figure had a rectangular body with no limbs featured. The head – on a slender neck – had a stylized face with schematic eyes, wedge-shaped nose and simple mouth in a style found on many Iron Age carvings throughout much of the Celtic world.[18]

The relative simplicity of the cemetery burials serves to emphasize the exceptional nature of the crowned burial. It has been described as one of the most important collections of metal artefacts from any Iron Age grave in Britain given the range and quality of the decorated objects.[19] In fact the whole complex and its chronological span, the crowned burial, the horse burial and the subterranean shrine, all imply that this region on the Kent coast was of special importance, and those who ruled it may have been equally distinctive.

There is a remarkable example of the rite of reversal in the 'princely grave' at Hochdorf (Baden-Württemberg, Germany). In this exceptional burial the corpse of a physically impressive adult male was laid on a bronze couch (Fig. 4.4).[20] He had been buried beneath a very large mound in a great timber and stone vault as a protection against grave robbers. It was evident that the funerary activity took several weeks and some five years may have passed before the construction of the mound was completed. It was a protracted and public affair in the mid-6th century BC.

The bronze couch, supported by eight castors in the form of female figurines, is a unique piece of funerary furniture and was modelled on north Italian fashions. The deceased was accompanied by the aristocratic status symbols common in graves of this type: a drinking and feasting set, a four-wheeled wagon and personal ornaments. The wooden wagon was a ceremonial vehicle clad in sheet iron. Harness fitments for two horses, nine bronze plates, three bronze basins (all showing signs of use presumably as feasting equipment), a heavy iron axe, a long iron knife and a socketed iron spike were placed

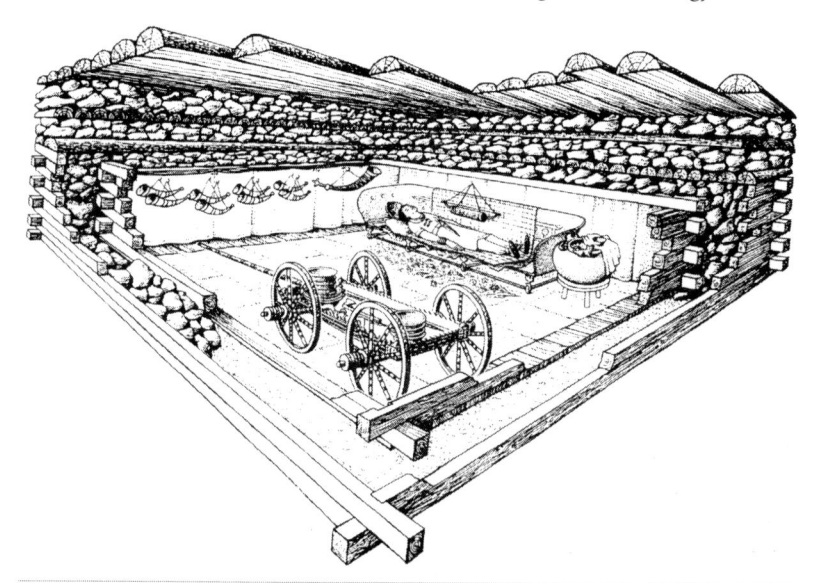

Figure 4.4. A reconstruction of the Hochdorf burial which had been placed in a great timber and stone vault. The body lay on a bronze couch supported by eight castors in the form of female figurines and was accompanied by the aristocratic status symbols common in graves of this type: a drinking and feasting set that included nine drinking horns, a four-wheeled wagon and personal ornaments.

on top of it. In addition to the horse equipment, equine symbolism occurs on the bronze couch where the decoration includes images of warriors in combat and paired stallions drawing a wagon. Nine drinking horns hung on the wall of the chamber, eight were made of cattle horn but the largest, hanging behind the head of the corpse, was made of sheet iron.

Other grave goods included a conical birch-bark hat, a broad collar of sheet gold, two gold fibulae, a gold armlet, a gold-covered bronze belt plaque and sheet gold decoration on the pair of shoes. There was also sheet gold decoration on the scabbard of an iron dagger. A large bronze cauldron of Greek type, made in southern Italy, and a golden cup were placed at the foot of the corpse; the cauldron had once contained high-quality mead. Craftsmen were summoned to the burial site to make some of the ornaments including strips of decorated sheet gold for the dead man's shoes. Golden shoes were a symbolic attribute of kingship in Irish and Welsh tradition and there is some etymological evidence in Old and Middle Irish that suggests shoes 'with uppers of gold' may have been marks of distinction.[21]

There was a particularly interesting example of reversal or inversion in this grave. The dead man's shoes had perished but the decorative golden attachments indicated that the right shoe had been placed on the left foot and vice versa and in all probability this was a deliberate act. There is an obvious difference between the wearing of shoes on the wrong feet and the wearing of just one shoe with the other foot unshod but it is possible that the rite of the single shoe or sandal, like reversed footwear, is another form of reversal or inversion.

There are early Irish references to Otherworld figures associated with a single piece of footwear. One wore one golden sandal which, as he walked, was on whichever foot touched the ground; another wore a silver sandal in a similar fashion and yet another wore a silver sandal on his left foot and a golden one on his right. As Proinsias Mac Cana suggested, this may be a motif in some way related to the Indian taboo that prohibited a king treading the ground unshod lest his potency be drained away into the earth but in early Irish tradition its supernatural associations are not in doubt.[22] There are some references in Classical literature and art to what has been called *monosandalisme* and it seems to have magical significance denoting a critical transition from one state of being to another. The rite of the single shoe emerged as an element in lordly inauguration ceremonies in Gaelic Ireland in the fifteenth and sixteenth centuries. A shoe was placed on the foot of the chief-elect or in one recorded case cast over his head (Chapter 6).

The Hochdorf person's shoes and the traditional high-status grave goods are not the only indication of his prestigious nature. The bronze couch is decorated with stylized images of warriors and ceremonial wagons drawn by stallions and these scenes may conceivably allude to his sacred obligations. The gold collar on the Hochdorf body was clearly an important object too for it had been deliberately cut with a sharp implement in what presumably was an act of de-consecration. Also significant, surely, is the fact that it bears equine symbolism.

4. Kings in Archaeology

Four very narrow zones of stamped images of winged horses forming a continuous frieze are placed in pairs of parallel bands one above and one below the mid-point of the collar. Edged by equally narrow zones of geometric motifs, the paired bands of horses are mirror images of each other. This is the only gold item to bear anything other than abstract motifs and miniaturization is unlikely to be an inconsequential detail. As Miranda Green has said depicting a winged horse (as on the Breton coin illustrated in Fig. 7.2, 4) may be a reference to the animal's Otherworld status for in many traditional societies flight is the mechanism by which a shaman or ritualist reaches the spirit-world.[23] Thus the Hochdorf collar might not just be a mark of rank but, with its inverted imagery, an indication of the Otherworldly source of this individual's power.

The question of the social standing of the Hochdorf 'prince' has, of course, led to much deliberation and a number of writers have alluded to the sacral character of such 'princely' persons. Dirk Krausse has argued that the iron axe, knife and spike found on the Hochdorf wagon close to the bronze plates and basins form a set of tools related to these eating utensils. Since iron axes have been found in other rich graves, he believes that it and the spike and knife were not just butchery equipment but implements for the sacrificial killing of animals and an indication of the religious status of the deceased.[24] Stéphane Verger, in an ambitious and complex analysis of various aspects of the contents of the grave, has suggested that the feasting and drinking equipment in the grave had diverse purposes and symbolic significance.[25] Since different types of plates were present, they may have been allocated to different persons. However, drinking ceremonies were dissimilar in his opinion because here the only significant variation was between the one large iron drinking horn and the eight other smaller organic ones. This, he thought, indicated a certain equality among those assembled for drinking rites, and he suggested the great iron horn was a communal drinking vessel on these occasions.

Irish evidence indicates the number nine might have a particular importance. The Rees brothers, in a study of the significance of numbers, have shown how early Irish literature has many references to 'companies of nine' sometimes consisting of a leader and eight others. In *Fled Bricrenn* (Bricriu's Feast) with its competition for the champion's portion, eight swordsmen guarded Bricriu on his way to the feast.[26] Lóegaire king of Tara commanded nine chariots to be equipped as he prepared to challenge Saint Patrick. The latter reference occurs in Muirchú's life of the saint written in the 7th century in which the pagan king is unflatteringly compared to Nebuchadnezzar of Babylon. As he prepares to confront the saint Lóegaire ordered 'nine chariots yoked therefore according to the tradition of the gods' (*Iunctis ergo nouem curribus secundum deorum traditionem*). His meeting with Patrick is probably the stuff of legend but Muirchú's allusion to a pagan belief in the symbolic importance of a gathering of nine warriors is revealing.[27] It is an arrangement that also occurs in the *Iliad* where Menestheus and Hector each go to battle with eight companions.[28] Here archaeology illuminates myth for the Hochdorf evidence indicates that this eight plus one configuration is an ancient element of European warrior ideology and not just a literary motif.

Verger believes that the wealth of goldwork and other insignia in the grave indicate that this man had acquired the sacral characteristics of kingship. The gold cup, found with the bronze cauldron, reflected his royal power sanctioned by the drink offered by the goddess of sovereignty (like the young woman in *Baile in Scáil* who granted rulership to Conn of the Hundred Battles). Whatever about his interpretation of the significance of the bronze plates and basins and of the nature of the drinking rituals and usage of the great drinking horn, he is right to stress the sacral character of the Hochdorf personage.

Remembering that story of the foundation of Massalia and the role of a sovereignty goddess-like figure who offered a bowl of wine to the chosen ruler, each drink of mead presented to the Hochdorf individual in his lifetime may have been a ceremonial re-enactment of his inauguration and an acknowledgement of his status. At the very least, the drinking horns and plates in the grave were, as is usually admitted, a part of a collective feasting set, but the very special status of the dead person may have been reflected in the deposition of nine particular items. While any attempt to reconstruct the social institutions of a prehistoric people must be a speculative exercise to a great degree, the concept of sacral kingship deserves to be a factor in the continuing discussion on the rank and role of exceptional personages like the Hochdorf male.

The Hochdorf grave raises one other interesting archaeological question. Some of the items in the burial such as a decorated belt plate and amber beads are objects often deposited in women's graves and might be considered more appropriate in a female funerary environment. The occurrence of ostensibly female ornaments in male burials has encouraged suggestions that they might denote the practice of 'ritual transvestism' or the presence of 'rule-breaking rulers' in Iron Age Europe. Early Irish literature offers some interesting insights in this respect. Rather than being a reference to the deceased's gender, the presence of essentially feminine items of adornment in a grave could be an expression of the ruler's all-embracing beauty. We know that an aesthetic of male beauty was an important part of warrior identity as early as the Bronze Age.[29] It was also an important element in the relationship between poet and patron in medieval Ireland. Fetishization of the beauty of a leader was a form of male homosocial bonding and great emphasis was often given to the lord's beauty, his attractiveness to men and the poet's desire to be by his side. Remembering the physical perfection demanded of a sacred king, the beauty of a ruler would be an expected feature of someone who is the flawless bridegroom of the goddess of sovereignty.[30]

There is an Indo-European dimension to this relationship of poet and patron. Mac Cana has written: 'That formal eulogy was regarded as central to the relation of poet or priest-poet and royal patron is evidenced abundantly in Celtic sources as it is in Indic and other Indo-European traditions, and in the light of the interpretative commentaries of modern Indo-European specialists – Dumézil, Benveniste, Gonda, Watkins and others – one might well say that in ancient times formal eulogy was the life-blood of sacral kingship'.[31]

If the Hochdorf burial offers us one manifestation of the sacred, the discoveries at the Glauberg may be another. This is a hillfort of Hallstatt and earlier La Tène date north of Frankfurt in western

Germany. One of two burial mounds to the south of the settlement was a huge monument some 50 m in diameter surrounded by a deep ditch. It was approached on the south-east by a pair of parallel 10 m wide ditches forming a processional avenue some 400 m in length – a feature that has been compared to the so-called Banqueting Hall on Tara.[32] A wooden chamber in this mound contained the corpse of an adult male with rich grave goods including a highly decorated bronze flagon that once held a honey-based drink, an iron sword and three spears, a bow with quiver and arrows, and a shield made of wood, leather and iron. Gold ornaments included earrings, a bracelet, a finger ring and a torc.

A life-sized sandstone statue of an adult male, found beside the mound on the north-west, was an exceptional discovery, and fragments of several other statues have been recovered as well. The large figure is depicted wearing leather body armour, carrying a sword and shield and wearing several bracelets, a finger ring and a torc that closely resembles the one found in the grave nearby.[33] This seems to be an image of the man buried there (Fig. 4.5). Rich in symbolism, this statue has been called a warrior, a stone knight, a hero, a mortal or a god. The prominent leaf-crown is a well-known motif in Celtic art and many writers have considered it a symbol of divinity.

There is an obvious difference in the representation of the upper and lower body of the Glauberg figure. The arms are simply carved and relatively narrow, the right held in a ritual pose, hand on chest with thumb upright. The legs are well defined, the heavy thighs in particular recalling the athletic and naturalistic style of Greek *kouros* statues. It may be that some of the attributes of a sacral king are encoded here, the stylized arms and short sword and small shield representing the controlled power of a just ruler, the strongly delineated thighs and calves evoking his relationship with strength and fertility. The position of the right hand recalls the similar gesture on the Capestrano figure (Fig. 4.1) where the right arm, with raised thumb, also lies across the chest.

In contrast, the well-known statue of a naked male from Hirschlanden (Baden-Württemberg) has his left arm in a similar pose

Figure 4.5. Life-sized stone statue found at the Glauberg.

with raised thumb. Naked but for a conical hat (like that found with the Hochdorf male), a neck-ring, dagger and belt, its arms and legs are carved in the same contrasting Glauberg manner. Clearly phallic, its fertility symbolism is clear. The significance of the right-hand or left-hand gesture is uncertain but it is an interesting possibility that the left-hand pose might have feminine connotations.[34] If so, the Hirschlanden statue might be seen as combining the feminine and masculine elements of sacral kingship in a very expressive way. It is also interesting to note that this left-hand gesture (with prominent raised thumb) is also evident on a carved relief of a *cakravartin* or world king from Jaggaiahpeta, Andhra Pradesh, in south-eastern India, dated to around the 1st century BC. It is worth noting too that his feet do not touch the ground for he stands on a cushion – recalling the taboo against a king's feet touching the earth.[35] Both the Glauberg and Hirschlanden statues are almost complete but both now lack their feet. The missing feet are puzzling and maybe both statues once had their legs simply inserted in sockets in something that raised them above the ground. Alternatively, if their feet were shod, then since their shoes may have been especially symbolic, their removal might mark the decommissioning of the powers of a sacral individual.

Irish tradition may offer an explanation for the unusual prominence of the thumb in these different male figures. The thumb may be a symbol of wisdom. In the tale *Macgníomhartha Finn* (The Boyhood Deeds of Finn), the legendary warrior Finn mac Cumaill famously acquired supernatural knowledge and prophetic power when he placed his thumb in his mouth having touched a magical 'Salmon of Knowledge' from the River Boyne. Finn's 'Thumb of Knowledge' figures in several stories: in one he catches his thumb in the doorway of an entrance to the Otherworld on the summit of the Curlew Mountains in north-western Roscommon and again puts it in his mouth with similar results. A version of this rite is recorded in folklore and in the late tale *Cath Finntrágha* (The Battle of Ventry). This 15th century text, containing older material, has Finn chewing his thumb: 'he put his thumb in his mouth and chewed it to the bone, and from there to the marrow and from there to the marrow heart and knowledge was manifested to him'. The peculiar formula of enumerating body parts in this fashion has an Indo-European ancestry.[36]

The motif of a thumb in the mouth supplying knowledge is to be found in Nordic mythology where the hero Sigurd (the son of Sigmund who drew the sword from the tree) kills the dragon Fafnir, roasts its heart and burns his thumb in the process. When he puts his thumb in his mouth, he gains the wisdom to understand the language of the birds. In a very different medieval context, two seated or squatting figures with thumbs in their mouths are depicted on an early Christian cross slab from Drumhallagh, Co. Donegal.[37] It is unlikely that this is meant to be Sigurd who, however, is depicted with thumb in mouth on a wooden panel on the portal of a stave built church at Hylestad now housed in the Museum of Cultural History, Oslo (Fig. 5.4). This scene of the dragon-slayer acquiring knowledge is to be found in quite a number of other carvings in wood and stone and on several cross slabs in the Isle of Man and on a high cross at Halton, Lancashire, for instance.[38] In ancient Rome the belief that the thumb was associated with power, and the fact that it played a prominent role in preparing medicines and effecting cures, may be a variation on this notion of wisdom.[39]

The range of symbols on statues such as Glauberg and Hirschlanden – and indeed the Capestrano warrior – would appear to embrace concepts such as exalted status or divinity, martial capability, wisdom and fertility. That they might be representations of sacred individuals is worthy of serious consideration. While flamboyant burials like Hochdorf are promising subjects to study in the search for elite persons like sacral kings, such rich and superbly excavated graves are not a widespread phenomenon in any period. Even though a number of very wealthy graves are known in the later Bronze Age (and some in central Europe have even been described as royal burials) the practice of cremation and a tendency to consign grave goods to a funeral pyre makes analysis difficult. Some of the rich late prehistoric 'princely' graves of southern Iberia were probably kingly burials and have provoked the suggestion that they may reflect the presence of 'sacred monarchies' in the 8th–6th centuries BC.[40]

Richly furnished graves of the earlier Bronze Age should not be ignored either as they sometimes contain objects that may well have been symbols of individual power. These offer good evidence of social stratification in the early 2nd millennium BC. The rich burials of the Únětice world in Central Europe represent one regional elite at this time. The huge tumulus at Leubingen in Thuringia is one example dated to approximately 1900 BC. It was investigated in 1877 and measured some 34 m in diameter and 8 m in height. Beneath it, a timber mortuary house covered a male burial accompanied by a wide range of objects. Some poorly preserved bones, possibly of a child, lay across the male corpse. Personal ornaments in gold associated with the man comprised a spiral bead, two hair or finger rings, two large pins and a large arm ring.

In a study that reminds us of the complex messages that may be encoded in grave goods, Marie Louise Stig Sørensen suggests other items in this grave might be more or other than individual possessions. These comprised a storage jar, a large polished perforated stone pick or hoe and a whet stone – perhaps connected with agricultural practices or metal working, a halberd, three small knives, two flat axes, and three chisels that were presumably wood-working tools. Some of these may not have been a reflection of what this man did in life but a reference to a range of productive tasks and spheres of activity with which he was associated.[41]

Similar graves in Brittany – where human remains rarely survive the acidic soils – contain objects of high value in both quality and quantity. Noteworthy are silver cups from two of these burial mounds, a form replicated in gold and amber in Britain.[42] These exceptional objects may indicate a practice of aristocratic, even sacred, drinking rites. Of course, there are other exceptional objects that indicate the presence of an elite. The unusual gold cape from Mold in Flintshire is an obvious case. Later gold items such as the golden hats from Ireland and Spain and the ceremonial headgear, the so-called golden crowns, from Germany and France may tell a similar story.[43]

The famous Bush Barrow burial near Stonehenge is a well known British instance of an elite burial (Fig. 4.6).[44] This large burial mound, 49 m in overall diameter, was dug in 1808 and found to cover an unburnt human skeleton possibly flexed and presumably male, accompanied by rich grave goods. These included two lozenge-shaped gold plaques, a gold covering for a belt hook, a bronze axehead, several bronze daggers – one with a hilt elaborately ornamented with almost microscopic gold wire-like pins, and a stone macehead with a decorated shaft. The high status of the individual buried here is not in doubt. The gold work, notably the larger lozenge-shaped piece with finely engraved geometric ornament, is of extraordinary quality. As many as 60,000 to 70,000 minute pins may have decorated the dagger hilt. Outstanding technical skill of this sort indicates an extravagant interest in technical virtuosity presumably to indulge the aesthetic demands of a patron. Exotic metals like gold, amber and silver were spiritually powerful materials, and fine metalwork with an emphasis on intricacy (to use Stuart Needham's phraseology)[45] was one of the marks of an elite minority.

4. *Kings in Archaeology* 77

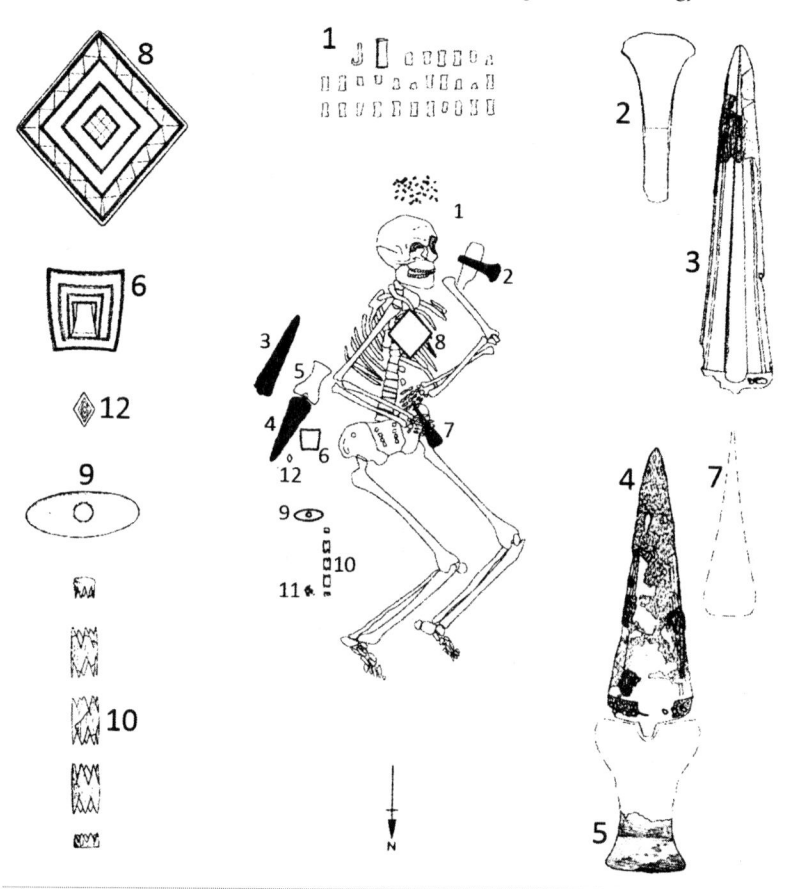

Figure 4.6. Reconstructed plan of the Bush Barrow burial dug in 1808. The principal grave goods included two gold plaques (8 and 12), a gold belt-hook (6), a stone mace-head (9) and bone mounts (10), a bronze axe (2) and two daggers (3 and 4), one with a gold decorated hilt (5).

Of course exotic objects may not be indices of sacrality. As ethnographic analogy reminds us, such significance might be marked in life by modest artefacts charged with symbolism such as a fly-whisk, a shell necklace or a bead head-dress. Indications of this elusive sacral dimension, if such there be, may change over time and from place to place. It is fair to assume that any item in a grave, even one in a fragmentary condition, may be significant. As we shall see in the case of inverted pottery, their placement may have symbolic connotations too. The study of the sequence of activities in the burial process may reveal clues as well and it is undoubtedly true that a focus both on the actions involved and on the objects included may be a rewarding approach.[46]

Funerary evidence may not be the only route to engaging with this challenging topic. Some settlement patterns may be worth analysing too. For instance, the Iron Age brochs of Atlantic Scotland are substantial structures that stand in sharp contrast to other contemporary settlement forms. Niall Sharples makes the interesting point that their occupants may have had a role in their local community that set them apart socially and geographically from the rest. He suggests that status – perhaps linked to a range of activities including the acquisition of ritual acknowledge – may have been transferrable from one incumbent to another.[47] If so, this individual could well have been invested with sacral qualities.

Exceptional burials like Bush Barrow, whether in England, Brittany or central Europe, do denote the emergence of leaders or lineages able and willing to express their status through funerary displays at an early date.[48] The nature of these elite individuals remains a matter of debate and terms like chiefs and princes are occasionally used. The richest graves share many puzzling features, not least the fact that they represent episodes of funerary extravagance that are relatively short, just several centuries at most. This has raised questions about the longer term nature of the development of society and social forms in prehistoric Europe. Even allowing for the likelihood of significant regional variations at any particular time, the overall picture provided by archaeology in the Bronze Age and Iron Age appears to suggest a rather dramatic oscillating pattern rather than any neat linear development to greater complexity (Fig. 4.7).

The disappearance of a rich burial tradition has naturally enough prompted suggestions of dynastic collapse or dramatic social change and this, at times, may well have been the case. If these elites had an enduring sacral dimension, however, their power and influence

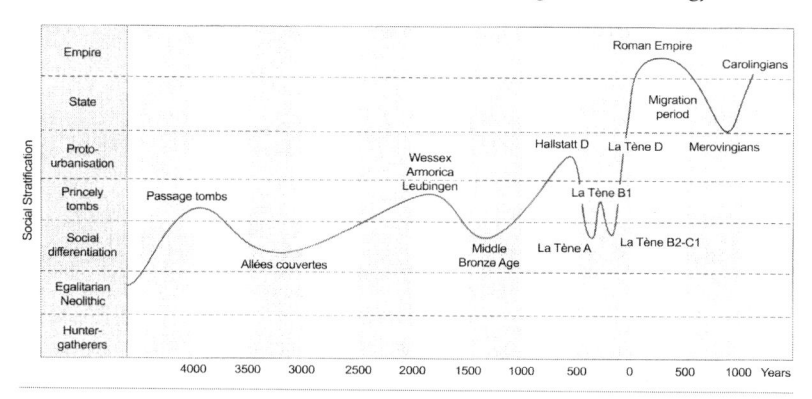

Figure 4.7. Real or illusionary? A representation of an oscillating pattern of social stratification in prehistoric Europe with the evidence for the early medieval period also shown.

may actually have persisted, manifesting itself in the archaeological record in a less flamboyant way if at all. Sacral leaders, supernaturally ordained, may not have had to express their special status in any particular fashion. Quite simply, rich possessions or larger dwellings may not have been necessary in lives circumscribed by ritual and, to some extent, this oscillating picture presented by archaeology may be illusionary.

CHAPTER 5

The Otherworld

The Otherworld is a prominent theme in early Irish tradition and Rathcroghan stands apart from other royal sites in Ireland in possessing an entrance to this supernatural realm. One medieval writer called it 'Ireland's gate to Hell' in the early 9th century tale *Cath Maige Mucrama* (The Battle of Mag Mucrama). This, the cave of Crúachain, today called Oweynagat (the cave of the cats), is a medieval souterrain attached to a long natural limestone cave and it is possible, with a little difficulty, to enter it today.[1] Though a quite inconspicuous monument, it has a remarkable body of associated myth and legend. Not surprisingly, perhaps, it is a 'thin place' now favoured by neo-pagans and seekers of spirituality alike.

In great part the medieval story of the Battle of Mag Mucrama is that of Lugaid mac Con, that unfortunate predecessor of Cormac mac Airt as king of Tara, but it also explains the name of the battle site which is the plain of the counting of the pigs near Athenry, Co. Galway. The tale records one of several legends associated with the Roscommon cave:

> Now Mag Mucríma [was so called from] magic pigs that had come out of the cave of Crúachain. That is Ireland's gate to Hell. Out of it too came the swarm of three-headed creatures that laid Ireland waste until Amairgene father of Conall Cernach, fighting alone (?), destroyed it in the presence of all the Ulaid.
>
> Out of it also had come the saffron-coloured (?) bird-flock and they withered up everything in Ireland that their breath touched until the Ulaid killed them with their slings.
>
> Out of it then had come these pigs. Whatever [land] they traversed no corn or grass or leaf grew on it until the end of

seven years. Wherever they were being counted they would not stay there but would go into another territory. If the attempt to count them succeeded the counts did not agree, for example: 'There are three of them', said one man. 'There are more, seven of them', said another. 'There are nine of them', said another. 'Eleven pigs', 'thirteen pigs'. Thus it was impossible to count them. Nor were they able to slay them for when cast at they disappeared.

On one occasion Medb of Crúachu and Ailill went to Mag Mucríma to reckon them. They were counted by them then. Medb was in her chariot. One of the pigs jumped across the chariot. 'That pig is an extra one, Medb', said everyone. 'It won't be this one', said Medb, seizing the pig's shank so that its skin split on its forehead and it left the skin in her hand along with the shank and it is not known where they went from that time onwards. It is from that Mag Mucríma is [named].[2]

In this story a band of supernatural wild pigs that cannot be counted emerges from this underground place and wreak havoc and destruction on the surrounding land. They cannot be killed but counting them, it is said, would make them depart. This, however, turns out to be impossible but when Medb and Ailill attempt this, one pig jumps over their chariot, the queen grabs a leg and the pig leaves it in her hand together with its skin. As a result, the malicious swine disappear forever. This act, bizarre though it might seem, portrays Medb and Ailill in their sacral function of protecting the land.[3] Though placed in a non-Christian past, this aspect of myth and its depiction of righteous rule would still have had a very pertinent meaning in the real world of early medieval Ireland.

There are other meanings in this story too. The war-goddess the Morrígan, monstrous cats, and a swarm of triple-headed animals are amongst other fearsome entities associated with this famous cave. These tales of destructive pigs and other creatures are echoes of the cave's links with the powers of chaos and are an illustration of the negative aspects of the Otherworld in Irish tradition. The malevolent forces of this world are prone to emerge at the great feast of Samhain (1st November). This was the traditional end of summer (*sam*) and the beginning of winter, a point in time when the juncture between this world and the other was so insubstantial that supernatural beings might invade the world of men. The terrors of the eve of Samhain find echoes in more recent times in the folklore of Hallowe'en when spirits walk abroad.

While the image of a blissful Otherworld captured the poetic imagination of Yeats, the dark side of this magical realm is easily overlooked. It has a powerful metaphorical purpose in any consideration of sacral kingship. In locating a hazardous entrance to the Otherworld close by a royal settlement at Rathcroghan, medieval writers might easily be accused of remarkably bad planning, but they had serious reasons for doing so. Here two features in the landscape, the cave and the royal house, are used to express a fundamental truth. The Otherworld signifies disorder, the king represents cosmic order and good fortune.

Why this quite unremarkable cave and souterrain should have gained such a remarkable reputation as an otherworldly entrance probably lies in the rituals that were once practised there. That Amairgene who killed the swarm of three-headed creatures is just one of several legendary warriors associated with this place. These links suggest this underground place may have been a location for warrior initiation practices involving isolation and deprivation.[4]

The horrors of the night of Samhain and the weird events that may happen then are also apparent in the very strange and surreal tale *Echtrae Nera* (The Adventure of Nera).[5] It begins:

> One Samhain night, Ailill and Medb were in Ráth Cruachain with their whole household. They set about boiling their food. Two prisoners had been hanged by them the day before. Then Ailill said, 'Whoever puts a supple twig around the foot of one of the two prisoners who are on the gallows, that man will have from me as a reward anything he wishes'.
>
> Now the darkness and the horror of that night were great, and demons used always to appear on that night. Each of the men in turn went out to try the night; and it was soon that they came inside again.

5. The Otherworld

'I will have the reward from you', said Nera, 'I will go out'. 'You will have my gold-hilted sword', Ailill said.

Then Nera armed himself well, and went out to where the prisoners were. He put a supple twig around the foot of one of the two prisoners. It came off afterwards – this happened three times. Then the prisoner told him that unless he put a special spike in it, even if he were there till morning, its own spike would not hold the looped twig shut. The prisoner said to Nera from the gallows, 'Well done, Nera'. 'Well done, indeed', said Nera.

'By your honour as a warrior, take me upon your neck so that I can drink a drink with you. There was a great thirst on me when I was hanged'. 'Come onto my neck then', said Nera. He climbed onto his neck. 'Where shall I take you?' said Nera. 'To the house which is nearest us', said the prisoner.

Then they went to that house. They saw something: a lake of fire around the house. 'Our drink is not in this house', said the prisoner. 'The hearth-fire is always raked here. Go on to the next house nearest to us', said the prisoner. They went there, and saw a lake of water around it. 'Do not go to that house', said the prisoner. 'There is never any water left over from washing and bathing, nor a tub with slops, left there after bedtime. Go on to the next house', said the prisoner.

'My drink is in this house, anyway', said the prisoner. He let him down onto the ground. He went into the house. There was used washing-water and bathing-water there, and he took a drink from each. There was a tub of slops in the middle of the house, and he drank from it and then spat the last mouthful from his mouth into the faces of the people who were in the house, so that they all died. Hence it is not good for there to be water left over from washing and bathing, or a hearth-fire that has not been raked, or a tub with slops in it, in a house after bedtime.

After that Nera carried him back to his torture, and returned to Ráth Crúachain. He saw something: the stronghold before him had been burnt, and he saw the heads of its people which had been heaped up by the warriors from the enemy stronghold. He followed the army into the cave of Crúachain ….

Myth and Materiality

The primary theme is the relationship between the two worlds at Samhain when journeys between the two are both easy and frequent. It provides us with some graphic pictures of this night's uncanny character. Sovereignty is another theme in the tale and even in the short passage quoted here there are allusions to what sovereignty must not be. It must not create disorder for instance and the dangerous slovenly house is a reflection of this as is Ailill's misjudged use of the warrior Nera as a servant.[6]

Having given an animated corpse a drink, we learn that Nera, on returning to Rathcroghan finds that an Otherworld army (the people of the *síd*) have burnt the court and left a heap of heads. He follows them into the Otherworld and finds a home and a wife there. His wife eventually explains to him that the destruction he witnessed was a vision and that Rathcroghan will really be destroyed the following Samhain unless its inhabitants are warned. When he asks how he will convince the court there that he has been in the *síd*, she tells him, in an important allusion to the inverted nature of the Otherworld, to bring the fruits of summer to the winter world outside:

> 'How will it be believed that I have gone into the síd?' asked Nera.
> 'Bring the fruits of summer with you', said the woman. So he brought wild garlic with him, and primroses and buttercups ….

He leaves the Otherworld to warn Ailill and Medb who eventually destroy the *síd* but Nera was left there together with his people and will remain there forever. John Carey has pointed out that the fruits of summer symbolize the mystery of Samhain: 'It is a time of intrusion, anomaly and reversal: that it begins the mortal winter is secondary here to its importance as gateway to the Otherworld summer. That the Irish should have named one of their most important festivals with reference to supernatural rather than natural time is striking testimony to the central position which the paradoxes of the Otherworld occupied in their vision of reality.'[7]

It is evident that when it is summer in one world, it is winter in the other. This sort of Otherworldy inversion is also alluded to in the early 13th century *History of the Danes* of Saxo Grammaticus. The king Hadingus or Hading has a bizarre experience:

As he was dining, a woman beside a brazier, bearing stalks of hemlock, was seen to raise her head from the ground and, extending the lap of her garment, seemed to be asking in what part of the world such fresh plants might have sprung up during the winter season. The king was eager to find out the answer and after she had muffled him in her cloak she vanished away with him beneath the earth. It was, I believe, by the design of the underworld gods that she took a living man to those parts he must visit when he died. First they penetrated a smoky veil of darkness, then walked along a path worn away by long ages of travellers, and glimpsed persons in rich robes and nobles dressed in purple; passing these by, they eventually came upon a sunny region, which produced the vegetation the woman had brought away. Having advanced further, they stumbled on a river of blue-black water, swirling in headlong descent and spinning in its swift eddies weapons of various kinds....

They cross a bridge and then witness two armies fighting each other in everlasting combat. They come to a wall and the woman cuts the head off a cock and throws it over the wall. The cock crows and lives and Hading abruptly finds himself in the real world again. This account may have been inspired by various sources – purple robes hint at Classical influence – but it is one of the most detailed accounts in northern literature of a visit to a pagan Otherworld.[8]

How can tales of an Otherworld like this possibly shed light on prehistoric beliefs? After all there may well have been a belief in an afterlife of sorts since the earliest days of humanity and this land of the dead may equally well have been perceived as a place of concord and harmony, even the opposite of this one. Around the world, it has taken many forms and has often been perceived as an idealized version of the real one but the concept of an inverted world is by no means as widespread.[9]

In early Irish literature it has many manifestations and it is also portrayed as a land of peace and plenty. It may be a land under the earth or the *síd* (otherworldly) mound.[10] The great mound of Newgrange was known as Brug na Bóinne (the Otherworld mansion or hall of the Boyne) and was the dwelling place of the Tuatha Dé

Danann including the great god Dagda and his son Óengus. In one tale called *De Gabáil int Sída* (The Taking of the Otherworld Mound) we are told that in the *síd* of Newgrange there is a wonderful land: 'There are three trees there perpetually bearing fruit and an everliving pig on the hoof and a cooked pig, and a vessel with excellent liquour, and all of this never grows less.'[11] The Otherworld may be an island, a place beneath the sea or beneath a lake.

In the 9th century *Echtra Laegairi* (The Adventure of Laegaire) the hero's journey takes him beneath a lake, Loch na nÉn, 'the lake of the birds', to a place of many attractions:

> Fine plaintive fairy music,
> going from kingdom to kingdom,
> drinking mead from bright vessels,
> talking with the one you love.
>
> We mingle a set of men of yellow gold
> on chessboards of white bronze;
> we have drinking of clear mead
> along with a proud armed warrior.[12]

This lake may have been located in Loughnaneane townland near Roscommon town and may be the place where that bronze cardiophylax was found (Fig. 4.1). This, of course, is just one example of the extraordinarily widespread custom of depositing hoards of metal objects or other materials in lakes, rivers bogs and in the earth itself. 'Votive offerings', 'ritual deposits', 'structured deposition', 'gifts to the Gods', are all terms used to describe a practice that reflects an extensive preoccupation with the powers of a netherworld.[13]

The Otherworld may be the abode of the dead and it has its sinister and malevolent aspects too. This darker aspect is very evident in the remarkable series of malevolent creatures associated with Oweynagat for instance. It was also a timeless region and, sometimes, the mirror image of the human world as the stories of Hadingus and Nera demonstrates. This and its essentially earth-bound nature are in marked contrast to the celestial paradise of Christian belief.

What is significant from an archaeological perspective is that its inverted quality may be reflected in prehistoric practices in those rites of reversal or inversion. We have seen this in the burial at Hochdorf where the shoes of the dead man were reversed and in the rich burial at Mill Hill, Deal, in which the sword scabbard and suspension ring were inverted (Fig. 4.3).

A series of late Bronze Age funerary or commemorative stelae in south-western Iberia are engraved with schematic motifs including stylized figures of warriors, swords, spears, chariots and circular shields. The shields are frequently shown not with their central frontal boss but with the rectangular handle or grip on the back of the object clearly depicted (Fig. 5.1).[14] This back-to-front presentation may be an attempt to indicate that the warrior denoted by the weaponry now belongs to the Otherworld. The occasional depiction of a sword on the warrior's right (rather than on the left as might be expected in a right-handed person) may be another expression of this reversal. We see this on a much later coin of the Redones from the Rennes region (Fig. 7.2, 2) with an image of an armed and naked woman riding a horse, the woman is depicted holding a shield in her right hand and a dagger in her left. Again a weapon would normally be shown in the right hand. It is assumed that such a figure is a war goddess – and this reversal is possibly an allusion to her Otherworldly nature.

Some Iron Age swords in male graves in France and Germany have been found inverted on the body – the point towards the head, the hilt towards the feet. Information is often scanty but in one case, a burial from Cazevieille north of Montpellier (Hérault), the sword had been ritually broken in three pieces but the point was still laid towards the head of the corpse.[15] Such rites of reversal have been noted in several English Iron Age burials as well. As mentioned in Chapter 4, an exceptional burial at Kirkburn (K5), Yorkshire, contained a coat of iron chain mail that had been laid upside down and back to front on top of the corpse of an adult male so that the hem was across the chest and the shoulders over the legs (Fig. 5.2).[16] This burial, beneath a square barrow, contained a dismantled two-wheeled chariot including some chariot fitments and the dead man was accompanied by various

88   *Myth and Materiality*

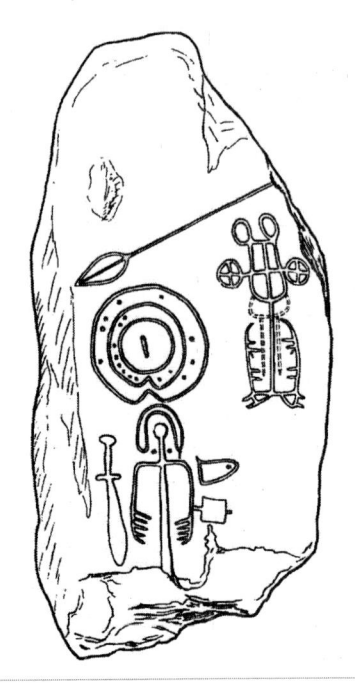

Figure 5.1. An engraved slab from Cabeza de Buey, Badajoz, depicting a helmeted warrior with sword, spear, shield and chariot; the shield is shown reversed with the grip rather than the frontal boss visible.

grave goods including some sort of organic container with bronze mounts on its lid, several bronze toggles, two bronze and iron horse bits and two deposits of pig bones.

The iron spines of some shields have been found placed face downwards in the grave suggesting the shield was laid face downwards. This was the case in another Yorkshire chariot burial at Wetwang Slack where a shield had been laid boss downwards on the corpse. An iron object, possibly the fitment for a wooden shield boss, in a second chariot burial there also suggested inversion.[17] Careful scrutiny of other funerary evidence may provide some more clues for a deeply rooted concept of an inverted Otherworld, a belief conceivably widely distributed in time and space and even reflected in the inversion of pottery vessels.

5. *The Otherworld* 89

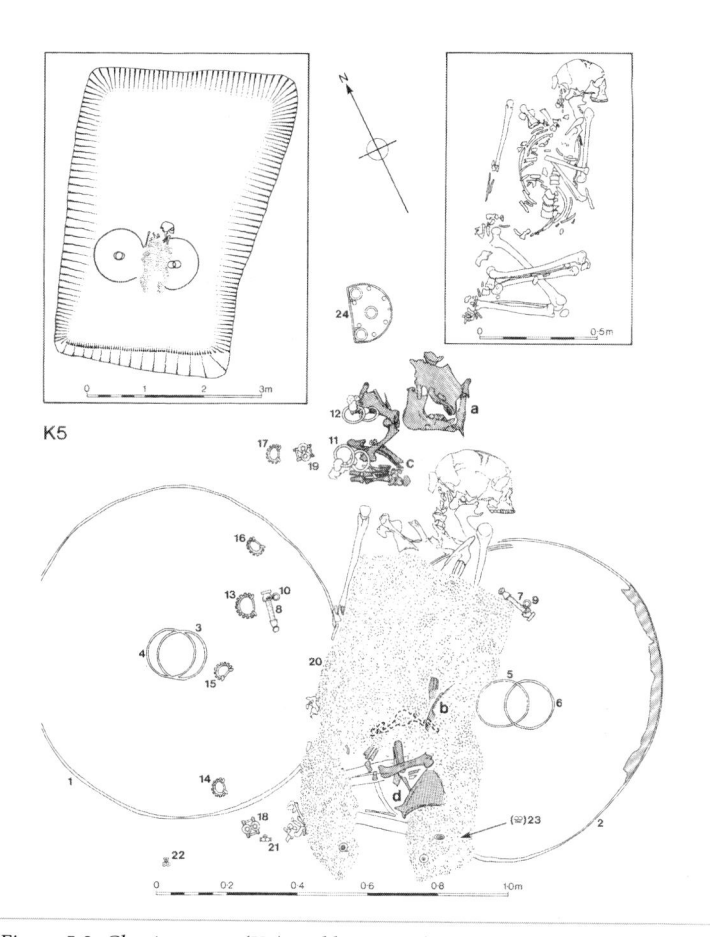

Figure 5.2. Chariot grave (K5) Kirkburn, Yorkshire. In addition to chariot fitments, an adult male was accompanied by various grave goods including an organic container with bronze mounts (24), bronze toggles (21–23), bronze and iron horse bits (11 and 12) and deposits of pig bones (a–d). A coat of chain-mail (20) was placed on the body and laid upside-down and back to front.

The inversion of pottery vessels in burials, either as accompanying vessels, as urns containing bones or as covering vessels, is a practice found at different times in various parts of Europe. It is particularly common in the British and Irish Bronze Age burial record for

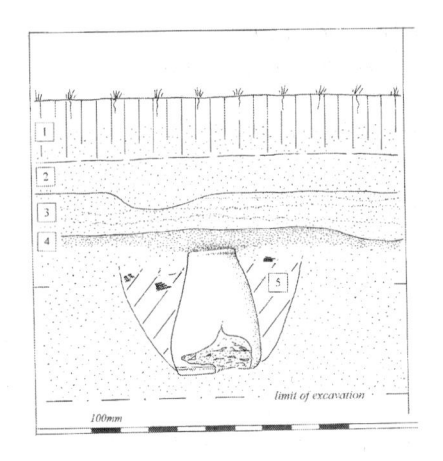

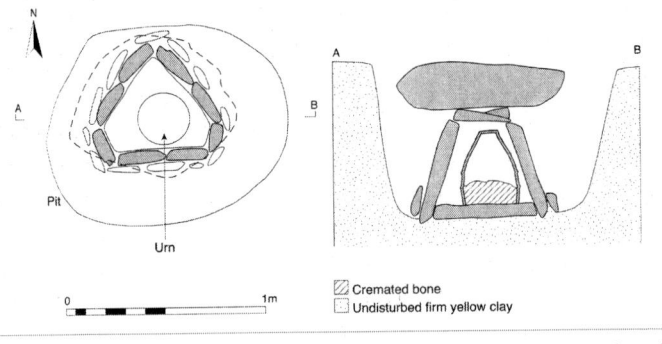

Figure 5.3. Inverted pottery. Above. An urn burial in a simple pit found at Findhorn, Moray. Below. An urn burial protected by a slab-built cist at Ballyvool, Co. Kilkenny.

example. Large cinerary urns containing cremated bone are often placed mouth downwards and sometimes empty vessels are also inverted in a grave. While it has been suggested that some larger vessels might represent a house of the dead,[18] it is fair to say that plausible house-like ceramic representations are not to be found. Some other symbolism is intended here.

Two finds may serve to illustrate this phenomenon (Fig. 5.3). One comes from Findhorn, Moray, in north-east Scotland, the other is an Irish urn burial from Ballyvool, Co. Kilkenny. The Findhorn urn, found in 1986, was like so many of these burial finds, an accidental discovery. It had been placed in a pit in a sand ridge and subsequently covered by an accumulation of sand. At first it was thought to be an old chimney pot and many months passed before it was eventually investigated. The mouth of the urn may have been covered by some organic material to retain its contents. This possible covering was represented by an organically-stained sandy layer. The inverted urn was a cordoned urn and was dated to between 1800–1600 BC. By urn burial standards, it was a relatively rich burial. It contained 23 faience beads and the cremated bones of an adult female, aged 18 to 25 years, and an infant either almost full-term or newborn.

Great care had been taken with the cremation and even the smallest of the infant's bones were included.[19] The glassy beads had been burnt on the funeral pyre and given the quantity they do suggest that this woman was a person of importance and her death, and that of her child, was considered a particularly tragic event. Because it had been inserted into a sandy pit, it could indeed be argued that the vessel was inverted to protect its contents. But this was not an insignificant and inadequately protected burial in a remote location. Across the Findhorn estuary from the Culbin Sands, this area was a sheltered coastal position and a key location for trade and exchange in the earlier Bronze Age.[20] The young woman buried here, and her child, were persons of some significance, and her burial was considered an appropriate one given her status.

The Ballyvool urn burial was found in 1946, and was well protected in a slab-built cist with a stone floor and a substantial capstone sealing the grave. The urn is possibly a vase urn and the cremated bones, examined at the time, represented 'at least one adult'. A sample of bone was radiocarbon dated in more recent times and indicates a date of approximately 1850–1830 BC.[21] The protection given to this burial would seem to suggest that the inversion of the urn had some other meaning and was not merely a covering for the bones. We can all too easily forget that this act of inversion was probably just one element, albeit an important one, in a protracted sequence of events. Here, as at Findhorn, the ritual performance presumably involved the preparation of the body, gathering material for the building of the funeral pyre, the burning of the remains and the sorting, selection and treatment of the ashes and bone. The digging of a pit or the sourcing of stones for a cist grave was just a further stage in a complex rite of passage. The site of the burial was possibly marked in some way and would remain the focus of acts of remembrance for some time to come.

Urn burial is a remarkably widespread tradition in the British and Irish earlier Bronze Age – some 2255 collared urns are recorded in Ian Longworth's 1984 corpus alone and, while details of burial are often lacking, inversion is by far the commonest practice.[22] It is a custom not confined to urn burial – so-called 'food vessels' have been found inverted from time to time as well.[23]

It is fair to say that it should no come as surprise that a belief in an Otherworld is a very ancient one. What is significant, however, is that the clues offered by Irish tradition may lead us to an explanation of some puzzling features of funerary practice. The inverted nature of this Otherworld may find expression in the archaeological record not just in the inversion or reversal of grave goods but in some solar symbols as well – as we shall see. It is an aspect of an ideology of the Otherworld that may be as old as the early Bronze Age if not older. Even though this custom of inversion or reversal is only detectable at very different periods and in very different places, it does suggest a widely held belief in former times. The prehistoric Otherworld is not as obscure and archaeologically elusive as one might think.

Reversed or inverted grave goods may not be the only funerary indication of this preoccupation with the passage of the dead between two very different worlds. The stone packing above a series of pre-Christian Migration period graves at Sylta, north of Stockholm, was carefully laid in a counter-clockwise direction and once again this reversal of the normal order, like reversed footware, would seem to be a symbolic allusion to the inverted world of the dead.

In a discussion of the Sylta phenomenon, Andreas Nordberg has drawn attention to the connection between some funerary practices and the necessity to perform some actions backwards, upside-down or contrary to the course of the sun.[24] He cites, for example, a scene on the 8th century picture-stone at Tängelgårda in Gotland

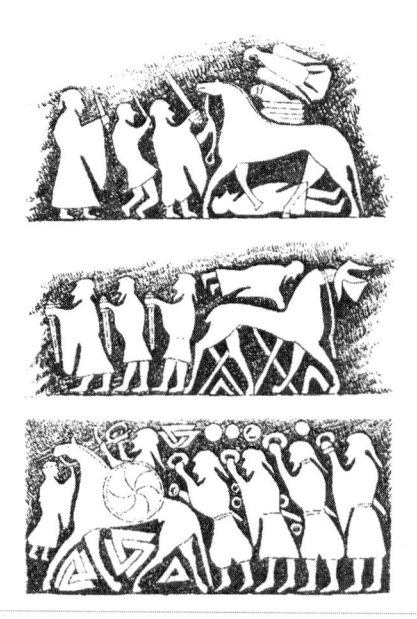

Figure 5.4. Scenes from Nordic mythology. Left. The central panel on a picture-stone at Tängelgårda, Gotland, depicts a funeral procession in which Odin's horse Sleipnir, with its eight legs, is carrying a fallen warrior to the Otherworld. Behind the horse, three men are walking backwards and carrying their swords upside-down. Right. An image (on the lower right) on a wooden carving from a church at Hylestad, Norway, shows the dragon-slayer Sigurd placing his thumb in his mouth upon which he gains wisdom and understands the language of the birds.

that depicts a funeral procession in which a horse with eight legs, Odin's horse Sleipnir, is carrying a fallen warrior to the Otherworld (Fig. 5.4). Behind the horse, which is wearing a hood over its head, the three men in the procession are walking backwards and carrying their swords upside-down. In the panel above three individuals are brandishing swords in a normal fashion. As he reminds us, death is a cosmic drama and the dead are often aided on their path between two worlds with complex rituals. From a mythic perspective their journey starts at the grave that is the portal to the next world. It provides, in an Old Norse context as in many others, an evident link between two worlds that may allow the dead to be consulted and certain practices associated with that Otherworld have to be carried out in a reversed fashion. Sylta indicates that reversal or inversion may be reflected in grave architecture as well.

The Otherworld may also be found if we follow the course of the sun. A belief that the setting sun descended into a netherworld may have been just as widespread in time and space. It seems that the inverted nature of this world below is represented in some solar symbolism too. This is a field of enquiry fraught with difficulty and sun symbols are often identified on the flimsiest grounds. Not every circle is an image of the sun. However, the question about the sun's nocturnal journey was very clearly asked in the early 12th century text *Immram Úa Corra* (The Voyage of the Uí Chorra). This is a story of the sea voyage of three brothers who when looking at the setting sun on the Atlantic coast in the west of Ireland asked a very pertinent question:

> One day, when they came forth over the edge of the haven, they were contemplating the sun as he went past them westwards, and they marvelled much concerning his course. 'And in what direction goes the sun', they say 'when he goes under the sea?'[25]

This mystery was once a real concern and it certainly preoccupied the medieval mind. It figures, for instance, in a section of a 9th century Old Irish apocryphal text *In Tenga Bithnua* (The Evernew Tongue). Here the spirit of the apostle Philip (whose tongue was cut out nine times and nine times miraculously regenerated) addresses the wise men of Jerusalem and explains the creation of the world to them. Here we are told that on the fourth day of Creation, God made 'the fiery circuit of the sun which … illuminates twelve plains beneath the edges of the world in its shining every night'. The sun shines on various places, some fearsome, some pleasant:

> First it shines on the stream beyond the sea, bringing it news of the waters in the east.
> Then it shines at night upon the lofty sea of fire, and upon the seas of sulphurous flame which surround the red peoples.
> Then it shines on the hosts of youths in the pleasant fields, who utter a cry to heaven for fear of the beast which kills many thousands of hosts beneath the waves to the south …

> Then it shines upon the dark tearful plain, with dragons who have been placed under the mist.
>
> Then it shines upon the flocks of birds who sing many songs together in the valley of the flowers ...
>
> Then it shines upon Adam's Paradise until it rises from the east in the morning; it would have many tales to relate upon its journey, if it had a tongue to disclose them.[26]

Some of the descriptions seem to derive from Gnostic writing in late antique Egypt but some such as the place peopled with 'flocks of birds who sing many songs' are reminiscent of aspects of the Otherworld in Irish tradition. The idea that the night-time sun passes through an underworld was clearly one of the mysteries of creation in medieval times.

There is good evidence, both literary and archaeological, that solar matters were of interest centuries before this. Saint Patrick, in his *Confessio,* declared 'the splendour of the material sun, which rises every day at the bidding of God, will pass away, and those who worship it will go into dire punishment', and even though the rest of the literary corpus is silent on the matter, this does suggest that the pagan Irish worshipped the sun. Archaeology offers supporting evidence that the sun had a role to play in their cosmological beliefs.

The Petrie Crown (Fig. 5.5) is so called because it was once in the collection of the 19th century antiquary George Petrie. We know nothing about its discovery and its provenance is unknown but like the bronze crown found on the skull of the man buried at Mill Hill in Kent it probably was a high-status or even kingly head-piece (Chapter 4). The Irish crown is fragmentary, now consisting of a band of openwork sheet bronze with a pair of slightly dished discs attached to the front. Each disc, some 5 cm in diameter, apparently supported a conical bronze horn, one of which survives. The band, the discs and the horn, are each very skilfully decorated with a symmetrical design of thin and elongated trumpet curves, some terminating in different sorts of bird's heads. It is usually imprecisely dated on stylistic grounds to around the 1st century AD.

The design on the disc below the surviving horn is the interpretative key because the bird's head terminals flank a circle set in a crescent

96 *Myth and Materiality*

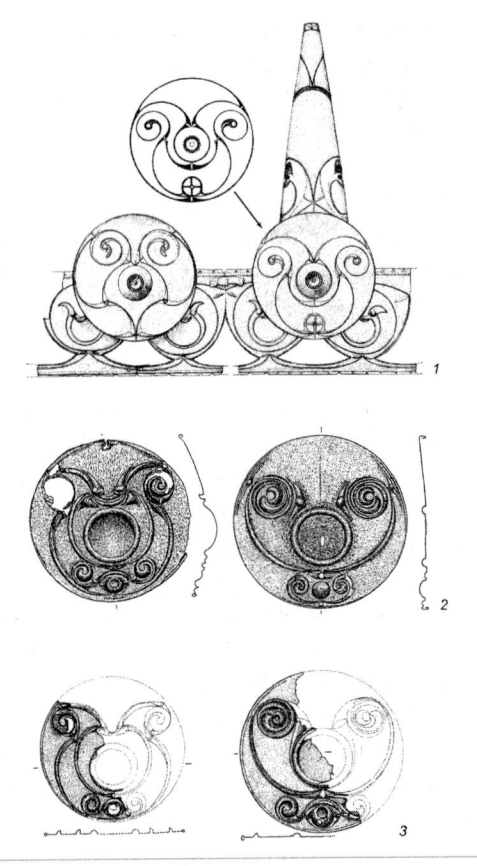

Figure 5.5. Solar imagery. 1. The Petrie Crown: a solar boat with bird's heads on prow and stern is depicted on the right-hand disc, reversed bird's heads occur on an openwork bronze band behind the discs and the solar roundel on the left-hand disc seems to be set in an inverted vessel. 2. Pair of bronze discs from Monasterevin, Co. Kildare: the stylized solar boat on the disc on the right has reversed bird's heads. 3. Pair of bronze discs from Co. Armagh: the stylized solar boat on the disc on the right also has reversed bird's heads. Various scales.

form. This is not, as was once claimed, a face with an upturned curling moustache[27] but a solar symbol. It is a representation of the solar boat with bird's head prow and stern. This ship that conveyed the sun across the sky appears in two different guises on the Petrie Crown and finds its clearest and fullest expression on this disc where a wheel motif in the boat and below the roundel gives emphasis to the solar symbolism. On the other disc the bird's heads and the roundel are well delineated but the boat motif appears inverted. There may be a great cosmological narrative represented here that also finds expression on a series of puzzling bronze discs.

A pair of these discs was found together at Monasterevin, Co. Kildare, and another possible pair comes from Co. Armagh (Fig. 5.5).[28] Made of sheet bronze, these discs are usually slightly concave and range in diameter from about 25 cm to just over 30 cm; their purpose is unknown. Decoration is similar but not identical and consists of bold repoussé work up to 10 mm high. The overall pattern is a fairly consistent one: a large central circle varying from a slight concavity to a deep bowl-shaped hollow lies within a symmetrical field of trumpet curves forming an approximately U-shaped or semi-circular arrangement with spiral terminals. Nothing is known about the circumstances of their discovery but their pairing is highly significant.

Once again it is a solar boat that is represented. Compared to the Petrie Crown, however, the designs on all these discs are more stylized and the paired bird heads are reduced to abstract curving features. In the past, the images on these discs would have been judged to be a severe case of stylistic disintegration. Not surprisingly, given the positioning of a pair of spirals above a circle, several writers have seen grotesque faces: 'great staring faces, enigmatic as so often in Celtic art'.[29] Another interpretation suggested 'while the ornament is essentially a geometrical fantasy, it is difficult not to see a grotesque face behind the fantasy'.[30] Paul-Marie Duval thought the design could be deliberately ambiguous, a face or an open-mouthed fish but Jope – in his characteristically austere approach – simply saw decoration derived ultimately from the palmette schema.[31]

The impressive craftsmanship of these Irish bronzes supports the notion that the designs they bear are especially significant. The degree of stylization suggests the artist was seeking to hide the solar symbol or perhaps trying to reduce it to its essential elements. In doing so they are giving greater emphasis to its inherent strength. This stylized image of the solar boat is not confined to Ireland – it

98 *Myth and Materiality*

Figure 5.6. Solar imagery. 1. The Battersea shield with solar imagery on lower roundel highlighted; the solar image on the upper roundel is inverted. 2. Aylesford bucket. 3. Unprovenanced Gibbs mirror. 4. Mirror from Aston, Herts. Various scales.

is to be found on British metalwork of the last century BC and the early centuries AD as well. It is a noteworthy detail on the celebrated Battersea shield (Fig. 5.6) where, along with swastika-like motifs, it is a prominent feature on the two smaller circular panels. It is to be found on the decorated bronze band on the Aylesford bucket where two pairs of bird-like creatures surround a whirligig. It occurs in an attenuated form on the unprovenanced Gibbs mirror and on the Aston, Hertfordshire, mirror. This motif, the 'lyre-loop with flanking coils' in Jody Joy's terminology, is the basis for the extremely complex designs on a number of other mirrors such as Birdlip, Gloucester, and Portesham, Dorset, as he has demonstrated.[32] On these remarkable pieces the solar motif has, it would seem, been deliberately hidden in an ornate composition.

These artists were now trying to do something very unusual. It seems as if they were deliberately trying to conceal or obscure the solar motif. This may have been a deliberate attempt to mystify the symbol, perhaps to make sure that it was only understood by a select few. They could have been trying to reduce it to its essential elements to give greater emphasis to its inherent strength. Alternatively they may have been deliberately introducing an element of ambiguity so those who saw grotesque human heads or faces in the discs, for example, could have just engaged in one potential reading.

There is another interesting possibility. The name of the god Lug means the bright or shining one and this has often been considered a reflection of his solar nature. Since it seems as if it may have been taboo to utter his name, perhaps a similar taboo applied to the overt depiction of his solar symbol? Lug may originally have been a god by whom people swore an oath. Thus a formula such as 'I swear to the god to whom my people swear' found in the Ulster Cycle was an oath (*lugiom* in Common Celtic) to a god whose name had to be avoided because others might learn to use it to their own advantage.[33]

The celestial voyage of the sun is not the only theme represented on these discs and on the Petrie Crown. The inverted boat on one of the pair of discs on the Petrie Crown is a reference to the world below as is the uppermost roundel on the Battersea shield which contains an inverted boat along with multiple swastikas. When the pairs of discs from Monasterevin and Armagh discs are placed side-by-side they too provide us with a graphic depiction of the cosmic story of the diurnal and nocturnal journey of the sun, one across the heavens, the other through an inverted Otherworld. The latter is signified by the reversed stylized bird's heads.

References to these two worlds, one often indicated by reversed or inverted motifs, is a part of much of the solar symbolism at an even earlier date in the Bronze Age. Images of people, animals and objects, in stone, wood or on bronze, are relatively rare in prehistoric Europe and where they do occur, they sometime provide valuable insights into aspects of the past about which we have little information. The Nordic Bronze Age has an exceptional iconographic repertoire on stone and bronze. This has enabled various writers to demonstrate the existence of a complex solar cosmography in which boats, solar imagery, human figures, horses and fish may figure.

The famous 'chariot of the sun' from Trundholm in Denmark is undoubtedly the best known Bronze Age solar symbol and it is one that tells a cosmic story. It very graphically illustrates the solar journey and the sacral function of the horse at this time (Fig. 5.7). The gold-plated bronze disc, mounted on a wheeled vehicle, is drawn by a horse from left to right and depicts the sun's westward route across the heavens in the northern hemisphere. When reversed and viewed from the other side, the back of the bronze disc, which was apparently never gold-covered, is pulled by the horse from right to left and this represents the sun's nocturnal journey under the land or under the sea towards the dawn in the east. It is a prehistoric answer to the question where does the sun go at night.

Among those who have explored the meaning of such symbolism, Flemming Kaul has shown that a cyclical solar story is illustrated on a series of bronze razors. A solar boat is sometimes depicted travelling from left to right, as the sun travels from east to west in its day-time journey across the heavens. When it is shown moving in the reverse direction from right to left, this represents its night-time journey through the underworld to its dawn in the east.[34] A razor from south Jutland displays an image of a boat containing two human figures, possibly twin solar deities, who are clearly paddling the vessel from left to right (Fig. 5.7). In contrast, an example from southern Zealand with horse-head prow and stern is sailing from right to left and is followed by a fish. Kaul suggests this is a ship of the night and the underworld and such left-sailing vessels, where they can be identified in Denmark, are never associated with solar images.

Horses and solar boats are regularly associated. According to Kristian Kristiansen complex mythological narratives are recognizable

5. *The Otherworld* 101

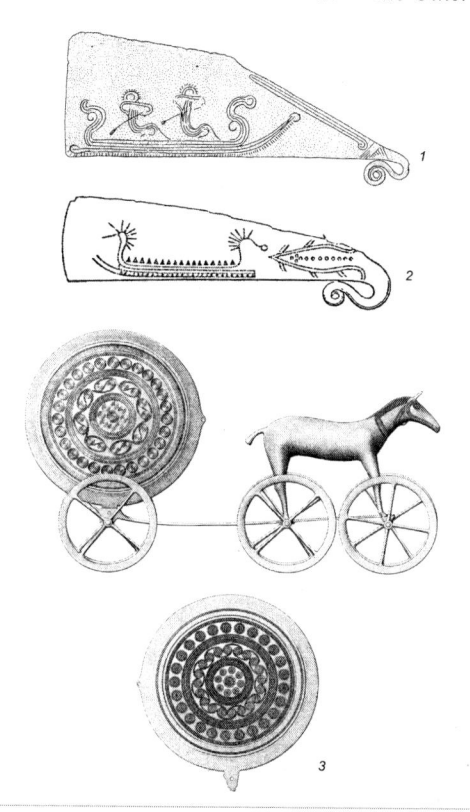

Figure 5.7. Solar journeys. 1. Bronze razor from south Jutland depicting a solar boat travelling from left to right and containing two human figures, possibly two aspects of the sun god. 2. Bronze razor from Møn, southern Zealand, showing a boat with horse-head prow and stern sailing towards the left followed by a fish. 3. The Trundholm 'chariot of the sun'. The gilded face of the bronze sun disc is drawn by the horse from left to right that is from east to west. The bronze face (below) is to the fore when the vehicle is drawn from right to left. Various scales.

in Scandinavian rock art. Solar boats are clearly identifiable with the sun represented by circles, wheels or cup marks. Some boats support horse's heads as on the images on bronze razors and some have horse figures associated with them. The presence of pairs of human figures may represent a Scandinavian version of the Dioscuri (the Greek

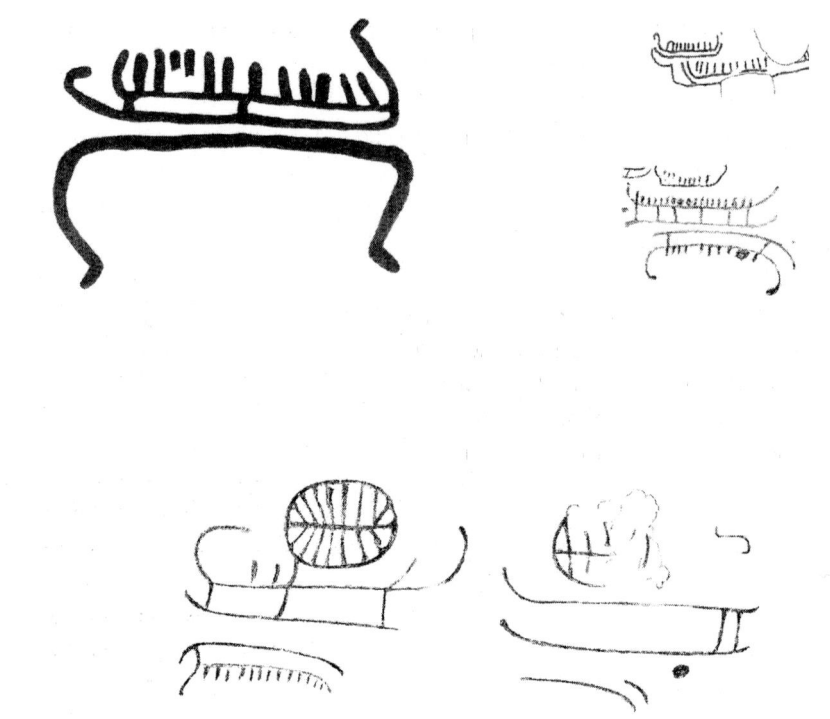

Figure 5.8. Images of upright and inverted boats in Scandinavian rock art.

exemplification of the Divine Twins of Indo-European myth). Some boats are sailing to the right and symbolize the sun's daytime journey, those sailing to the left depict its nocturnal voyage. This night-time journey through the underworld is also represented there by inverted boats. Sometimes upright and inverted boats are shown together representing upper and lower realms (Fig. 5.8).[35]

The role of the horse begins to undergo a fundamental transformation sometime around the middle of the 2nd millennium BC (Chapter 7). Its part in the cosmic drama of the voyage of the sun is replaced by magical birds. It is an interesting example how even symbols with a vital charge may undergo significant change. In the late Bronze Age in Central Europe we now find images of the sun disc set in a boat with bird's head prow and stern just as on those British and Irish Iron Age objects many centuries later. Some classic illustrations occur on a small number of bronze buckets of Hajdúböszörmény type in Hungary where the sun is shown as a disc or a boss prominently placed in a boat with duck or swan heads at either end (Fig. 5.9). One sheet bronze bucket bears embossed solar boat imagery in a broad frieze that circumscribes its upper body. The decoration on this, the Vienna situla as Stefan Wirth calls it, essentially consists of two zones of solar boats, one above the other, all sailing around the circumference of the vessel, in a continuous symmetrical composition that, in its mirror imagery, evokes the sun's journey above and below the horizon. As he points out, this is a cosmological narrative that recalls the different journeys of the sun.[36]

In certain cases the Otherworldly solar voyage is implied by reversal or inversion. In some designs, as on the Vienna situla and on a vessel from Nyírlugos, eastern Hungary, a central image is flanked by smaller boats with inturned bird's heads, the position of the sun being depicted as a small boss. These opposed or reversed birds are possibly intended to denote a nocturnal Otherworld ship and the complete image presents an abbreviated version of the story of the cosmic eternal return of the sun that affirms that day is not conquered by night.

The depiction of this solar theme on buckets such as that from Unterglauheim, Bavaria, found with a cremation and accompanied by two small bronze cauldrons and two golden cups, links this symbolism in very personal way with a prestigious individual. Wirth sees this as an expression of this sacral person's belief in their own divine power symbolically represented by the sun. He suggests the choreographed contrast between the cosmological symbolism on the bronze bucket and the transformation of the individual's mortal remains on a cremation pyre evokes, in the late Bronze Age, the concept of the dual nature of kingship well known to the medieval world, a monarch at once hedged with divinity but affected by human frailty.

As in Scandinavian rock art inverted boats on bronze objects may tell a similar Otherworldly tale. Unlike designs with reversed bird's heads, images of upturned solar boats are rare enough on bronzes, but they do occur. They are to be found, for example, paired keel to

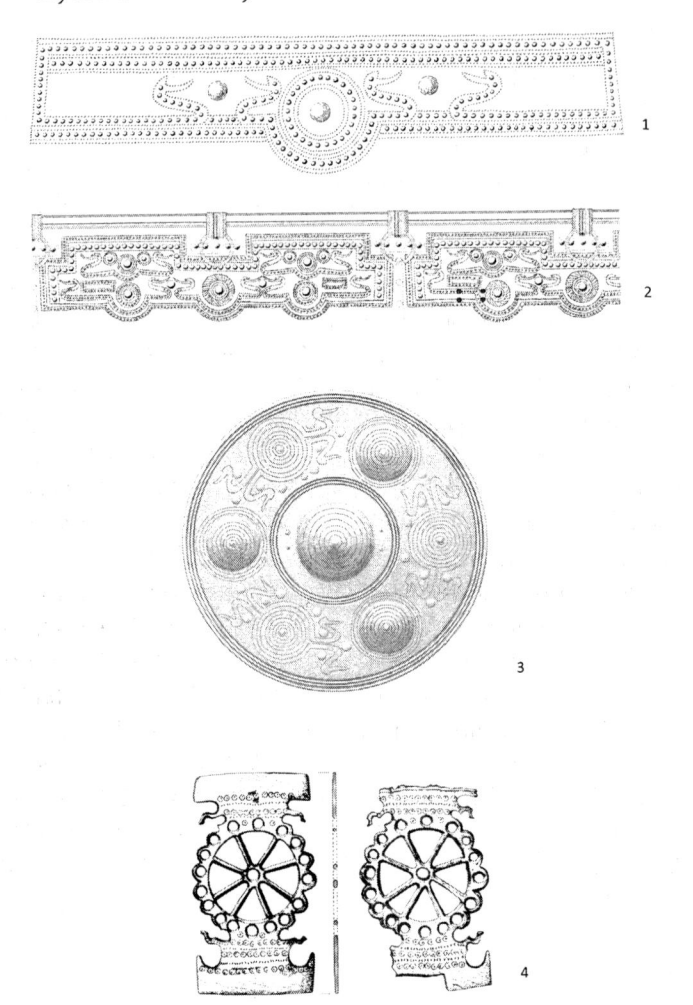

Figure 5.9. Solar images. 1. Detail of decoration on a bronze bucket from Nyírlugos, eastern Hungary, with a solar boat with bird's head prow and stern and sun disc flanked by smaller boats with reversed bird's heads. 2. The frieze of two rows of solar boats one above the other on the Vienna situla. 3. Three pairs of boats with bird's head prow and stern surround a solar disc on a bronze shield from Denmark. 4. Two of the bronze mounts on the wagon from the Vix burial with solar symbol and bird's heads. Various scales.

5. The Otherworld

keel with stylized upright craft in a frieze of embossed designs on a Hallstatt period bronze bucket from Kleinklein in Austria and on the plate of a bronze neck ring from Fangel Torp, Odense, Denmark.[37] Three pairs of boats with bird's head prow and stern surrounding a solar disc consisting of several concentric circles are depicted on a bronze shield from Denmark. Sets of small bosses serve to distinguish upper and lower boats (Fig. 5.9). This unique shield has no recorded provenance but its symbolism may have offered supernatural protection to its aristocratic owner.[38]

This design of pairs of birds set above and below a solar disc is to be found in the bronze plaques that decorated each side of the wooden superstructure of the wagon in the Vix burial in eastern France (Fig. 5.9). As already mentioned, this famous grave, excavated in the 1950s near Châtillon-sur-Seine, contained all the high-status symbols of the 5th century BC. The woman buried there may have been an exalted person with a role in the ritual serving of wine.

This Otherworldly symbolism, whether apparent in reversed or inverted grave goods, or in solar imagery, and found in such a wide variety of contexts and at different times in prehistoric Europe, is surely an expression of a remarkably widespread ideology. It may have been a universal belief even occurring in those many places where burials are not to be found or where imagery on stone or bronze was not the fashion. While its Bronze Age beginnings would seem to suggest that it is another element in Europe's Indo-European heritage, this notion of an inverted Otherworld may be as old as humanity itself.

CHAPTER 6

The Sacred Tree

The concept of the sacred tree has a remarkable longevity in Ireland and elsewhere. The *Annals of the Four Masters* record that Máel Sechnaill, king of Tara, laid waste the territory of the Dál gCais in Co. Clare in the year AD 982. He also provocatively felled the sacred tree at their royal inauguration site at Magh Adhair near the village of Quin in Co. Clare. In this contemptuous insult, the *bile* or sacred tree 'was cut after being dug from the earth with its roots'. This is an important detail: the tree was not simply cut down, its roots were deliberately dug up and exposed as well because, as we shall see, they too carried a symbolic charge. Such trees are recorded at three other inauguration sites in Connacht and in Ulster where the trees (*biledha*) of the Uí Néill at their inauguration place at Tullaghoge, near Dungannon, Co. Tyrone, were uprooted in 1111 AD according to the same annals. It was here that the inauguration ceremonial included the rite of the single shoe in which one shoe was placed on the foot of the chief-elect and also cast over his head.

Why these trees were so important is not clear but they may have had weighty mythological significance and symbolized age-old wisdom – and the 'rod of kingship', an emblem of legitimate royal authority, may have been cut from them.[1] In any event, all this points to some sort of association between tree and kingship ceremonial in medieval times. The Old and Middle Irish word *bile* means a sacred tree and there are many references to such ancient and venerated trees in early Irish literature. In particular five primeval sacred trees are often alluded to: Bile Tortan (the Tree of Tortu – an ash tree), Eó Rossa (the yew of Ross), Eó Mugna (the oak of Mugna – the *eó* element in its name here meaning great tree), Craeb Daithi (the bough of Daithi – an ash) and Bile Uisnig (the tree of Uisneach – an ash). The last mentioned stood somewhere in the great cult centre of Uisneach, Co. Meath, a cosmological central place and the centre point of the island of Ireland.[2] The Eó Mugna was said to have been hidden since the time of the great deluge, its appearance coinciding with the birth of a legendary king.

Their origins are recounted in the 10th–11th century text *Suidigud Tellaig Temra* (The Settling of the Possessions of Tara), a tale that is an amalgam of apocryphal and native features. Fintan mac Bóchra, the oldest man in Ireland and a survivor of the deluge, and a giant named Tréfhuilngid Tre-eochair meet to create the Irish landscape and divide the island into five parts. The latter carries a branch bearing three fruits and gives some of the berries to Fintan to plant, and from them grow the five sacred trees. Even though the Eó Mugna, that once stood in Co. Kildare, is described in *Airne Fíngein* (Fingein's Night-watch) as 'an offshoot of the tree in Paradise' implying that it sprang from the Tree of Life in the Garden of Eden, the mythical origins of all five suggest an older pagan ancestry.[3] The statement in the 8th century *Book of Armagh*, that a church was built beside the Bile Tortan at Ardbraccan, Co. Meath, implies the same.[4] A preexistent sacrosanctity was in all probability the determining factor for the construction of the early church thereabouts.

Five sacred trees are also to be found in the Hindu religious texts known as the Puranas that tell of the deeds of the gods and much else besides. They first appear at the churning of the cosmic ocean of milk by the gods (Devas) and demons (Asuras). One important tree called Pārijāta was stolen by the god Krisna and hidden for a period of time, an event that recalls the story of the Eó Mugna and a number of the other Irish trees.[5]

There are also tantalizingly brief references to special trees at two of the great prehistoric royal sites. In early legend, Cráebrúad, Red-branched, is the name applied to the great hall of the Ulster warriors at Emain Macha (Navan Fort). However this building is a medieval invention and the term more likely refers to a tree or a grove that once stood there. The name survives in the townland named Creeveroe adjacent to Navan Fort.[6] A fragmentary text in prose and poetry on the origin of the name of Tara mentions three walls on the summit of the hill built by the mythical Érimón, son of Míl. Dated to around AD 900, this brief account also refers to a great encircling rampart and 'a tree like a thicket having hundreds of crops' with, on one side, a branch bearing 'nine nuts on its top, an apple on its side'.[7] This fruitful magical tree was clearly noteworthy. There is a magical tree associated with Medb of Crúachain too though not at Rathcroghan. In the *Tain Bó Cuailnge,* as she pursued the bull of Cooley in western Co. Down and southern Antrim, 'every place where she planted her horsewhip is called *Bile Medba*' – a theme that has Classical parallels and recalls the many instances in the lives of Irish saints where a staff or crozier is planted and springs to life.[8] An archaic legal poem indicates that the felling of a sacred tree carried a fine of three cows.[9]

There is an enormous amount of folklore on remarkable trees not just in Ireland but around the world. Indeed in Ireland one folklore expert has written – almost despairingly – of such solitary trees: 'almost every tree growing in Ireland has a certain amount of traditional information associated with it'.[10] Thus it is no surprise to discover that special or sacred trees find archaeological and iconographic expression in ancient Europe in very diverse ways. Two different examples may serve to illustrate this variety and its great chronological range.

The Nidau-Büren canal in north-western Switzerland was dug in the late 19th century and in the course of its construction a late La Tène iron sword was discovered, probably at Port, Canton Bern, near the canal's junction with the lake known as the Bielersee. Many years later the sword, preserved in the Bern Historical Museum, was found to bear a remarkable inscription and punched design. Dated to the second half of the 1st century BC, the sword with its scabbard had been ritually decommissioned, being bent almost in two, and may have come from the bed of an old river. It bears the name Korisios in Greek script and above it, just below the hilt, the image of a palm tree flanked by a pair of rampant horned animals, possibly goat or ibex, seemingly eating from the tree (Fig. 6.1). This is the Tree of Life protected by an animal pair.[11]

The significance of an individual tree at a much earlier date is clearly demonstrated at Holme-next-the-Sea, Norfolk.[12] An oval setting of 55

6. The Sacred Tree

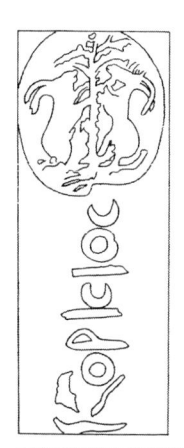

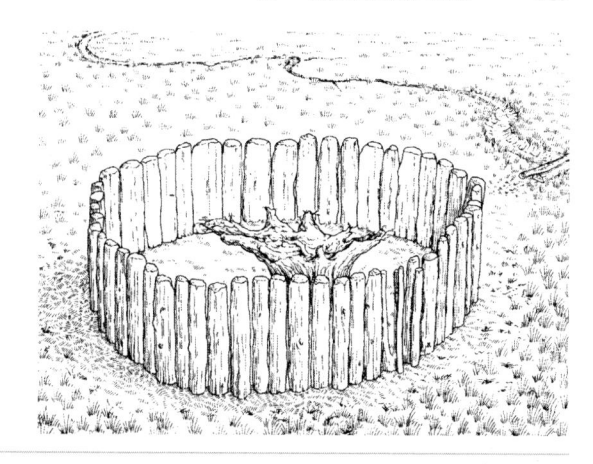

Figure 6.1. Sacred trees 2000 years apart. Left. Sketch of an image and a name on a 1st century BC sword found at Port in Switzerland. The name Korisios in Greek script is below an impression of the Tree of Life flanked by a pair of animals. Right. A reconstruction of the inverted tree set within a timber circle found at Holme in Norfolk and dated to 2049 BC.

large contiguous oak timbers with a maximum diameter of 6.78 m surrounded a pit containing the lower part of an inverted oak tree, its roots in the air. The end in the ground had been carefully trimmed and side branches and bark removed (Fig. 6.1). The Holme tree may have been toppled or blown over and dendrochronological analysis indicated the assemblage of timbers was felled in early 2049 BC. A number of the timber posts probably came from the central oak. The monument was constructed on the coast on a saltmarsh adjacent to intertidal mudflats and this exceptional waterlogged context ensured the survival of the timber structure. The large inverted oak was set in a pit 1.5 m deep with the remains of its roots deliberately exposed. Since pottery vessels in contemporary burials are often placed mouth downwards, it was suggested that this inversion in a liminal area may have marked the transformation of the tree from the world of the living to the world of the dead.

It is worth emphasizing that the Holme tree was uprooted and not simply cut down. Exposing its roots, and indeed the removal of its bark, had some particular symbolic significance. Noting that this took place early in the year, Francis Pryor wrote perceptively 'for practical purposes the period April to June is perhaps the worst possible time to fell a tree. The tree itself and everything around it is in full growth. No self-respecting forester would dream of felling timber at that time of year. But if the tree was seen as a symbol of life itself, then surely this would be the time to gather it in. It could be believed that its life forces were most vigorous in the spring and early summer. By inverting the tree in the ground, those life forces are being returned to the earth, the source of all life. The removal of the bark was the purification process that was needed before the tree could release its energies back into the ground'.[13]

The Holme tree was an exceptional discovery and it is no surprise that excavated evidence for special trees is almost non-existent. In Ireland, the burnt roots of a tree were found at the entrance to a small U-shaped ditched enclosure at Shanaclogh, in south Co. Limerick. A number of pits within the penannular enclosure contained cremated bone, and some coarse pottery sherds suggested a date in the middle Bronze Age. The excavator thought the tree was modern but situated as it was between the terminals of the ditch, the later suggestion that it might be the remains of a prehistoric sacred tree should be borne in mind.[14] More of these elusive objects may await identification.

The deliberate inversion of the Holme oak tree also suggests the tree itself had some special – even sacral – significance. Since the Tree of Life may extend from earth to heaven or from heaven to earth, this seems plausible. There are references to inverted sacred trees in early Indian and other traditions where the universe is conceived as a cosmic tree with its roots buried in the sky and its branches covering the whole earth.[15] The Holme tree may be an early material expression of a cosmological concept that had a wide currency in the Indo-European world and beyond.

In one account in Norse mythology, one of the three roots of the immense sacred ash tree Yggdrasill extended to the heavens, to the home of the gods. Yggdrasill, a name that is generally taken to mean 'Odin's Horse' which is a metaphor for a gallows because he hung himself from it for nine days and nights in the quest for knowledge. While several other sacred trees are mentioned in old

Norse cosmology, Yggdrasill is probably the best known European example of the world tree or *axis mundi,* the central metaphysical link between heaven and earth.

It has been argued that three-pointed stone settings found in considerable numbers in Sweden, Norway and Denmark are representations of the three roots of Yggdrasill that extended to other worlds.[16] These 'tree settings' or 'tricorns' may be built of earth, stone or a mixture of both. With concave sides, they often have a distinctive stone at the narrow pointed ends and some have a central monolith (Fig. 6.2). They are sometimes the focal monument in a cemetery. Some excavated examples have yielded simple cremated burials and are dated from the Late Roman Iron Age to the Viking Age (AD 200–1050). They are probably a development of simpler stone triangles with straight sides that generally date from the Pre-Roman Iron Age to the Migration Period (500 BC to AD 550). These too are associated with cremated burials but whether they have any tree associations is uncertain.

Given the exceptionally rich corpus of prehistoric rock art in Scandinavia, it is surprising that images of trees are relatively uncommon there. Where they occur, it has to be said, a schematic image of a tree is in itself no indication of a sacral dimension and there may be a mundane explanation. For instance, it may be that some trees with human figures attached are illustrations of tree management since not all rock art is necessarily the depiction of ritual activity. The collection of leaves and branches for winter fodder being just one possibility.[17] Moreover, not all brachiate images are necessarily those of trees: the branching lines and cup marks that form the so-called 'Tree of Life' motif in the rock art complex at Snowden Carr, North Yorkshire, have been compared to a small tree bearing fruit [18] but the intricate pattern combines elements common in local rock art and tree imagery is the least likely interpretation.

Some depictions of the Tree of Life are rudimentary to say the least. One crudely executed example, incised on a bronze Roman nail-cleaner, may have been a simple amulet. Found in Rivenhall, Essex, it is possibly dated to around the 4th century AD (Fig. 6.3). The design represents a less than impressive tree set in a rectangular receptacle flanked on the

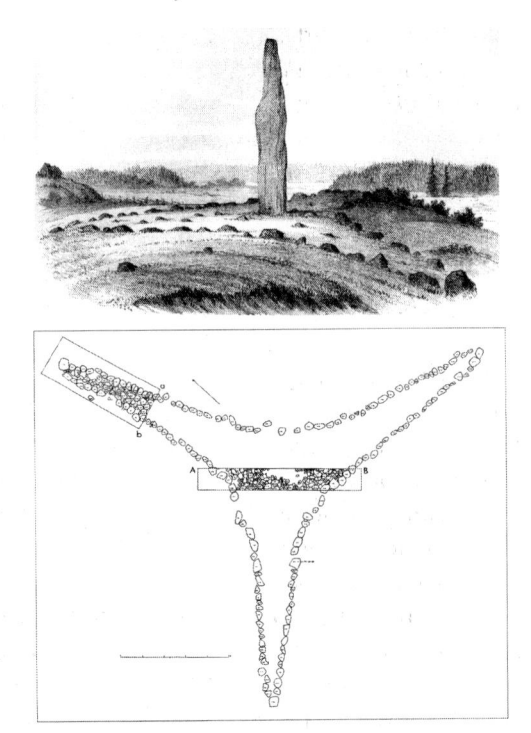

Figure 6.2. Scandinavian tree settings. Above. A three-pointed stone setting with a pillar stone in its centre at Herresta, Sweden, as recorded in the 19th century. Below. Plan of a three-pointed stone setting at Bjärsgård, Sweden.

right by a griffin and on the left by a peacock. It is a combination that foreshadows the wider representation of the theme in Christian art.[19]

A mushroom-shaped motif with a stem and a convex top occurs in Scandinavian rock art and on a range of bronze objects as well. Occasionally its top is bifurcated or it has curving terminals. Often depicted standing in a ship, it has been claimed to be a ship's mast with sail or a stylized representation of a sacred tree. However, the argument that it is meant to be an illustration of the curved blade of a ceremonial axe seems to be generally accepted.[20]

In Brittany, the sacred tree and *axis mundi* is a prominent and dazzling theme in the tale of the vision of the king Iudael (Chapter 3).

6. *The Sacred Tree*   113

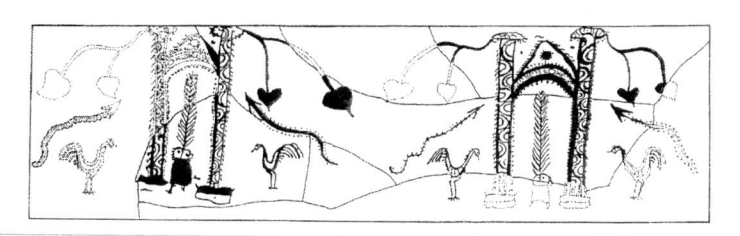

Figure 6.3. Above. A bronze Roman nail-cleaner found in Rivenhall, Essex, bears a crudely executed image of a sacred tree flanked by a griffin and a peacock. Below. A representation of temple-like structures with a tree springing from the head of a human figure on a pottery vessel from Arcóbriga, Spain.

It was a 'huge post in the form of a round column, founded by its roots in the ground, its mighty branches reaching the sky, and its straight shaft reaching from the earth up to the heavens'. To emphasis both its secular and religious importance, we are told that the post's lower part was of iron, its shaft decorated with iron pegs on which were hung swords, shields, spears and crested helmets, saddles, trumpets and more while the upper part of the post was of gleaming gold with gold pegs that supported Christian paraphernalia including censers, sacramental vessels and gospel books. At the end of each iron and gold peg were burning candles 'shining like stars perpetually'. As already mentioned it was situated in the very centre of Iudael's kingdom and Mac Cana thought that the differences between the lower and upper parts of the tree were meant to symbolically represent the two aspects of Iudael's life as warrior-king and saint.[21]

There is some intriguing and equally varied evidence from the Iberian peninsula. A Celtiberian painted vase bears a pair of images of a temple-like structure containing a tree springing from the head of small human figure. Found in fragments, the vessel comes from the settlement of Arcóbriga, near Zaragoza, in north-eastern Spain, and is dated to the 1st or 2nd century BC (Fig. 6.3).[22] This tree motif has prompted comparisons with tree-like motifs on some Gallo-Roman pottery from Lombez (Gers) and with other indications of a tree cult in the Celtic world.[23]

There is evidence of a very different sort from a more northern part of Spain. Sacred trees are recorded in medieval texts from the Basque country, from Guernica, Luyaondo and Arechabalaga that were gathering places of various kinds. Foremost among these was the Tree of Guernica, an oak that was the focus of assembly by the Lordship of Biscay (*Señorío de Vizcaya*) in the 14th century. Here they swore fidelity to the Basque *fueros* (municipal laws) and here the royal family of Castile (including Ferdinand and Isabella) swore to maintain the privileges of the Basque people. Here too, according to one account, there was an extraordinary echo of the rite of the single shoe (as practised at Tullaghoge). The investiture of the Lord of Vizcaya required his presence with one (left) foot unshod.[24]

Much has been written on the significance of sacred trees and groves in the Celtic world.[25] Many elements are well known including the description of Julius Caesar's destruction of a sacred grove near Marseille in 49 BC. Lucan's poetic account of this event in his epic *Civil War* (*Pharsalia*) presents a picture of a strange and sinister place:

> A grove there was, never profaned since time remote,
> enclosing with its intertwining branches the dingy air
> and chilly shadows, banishing sunlight far above.
> In this grove there are no rustic Pans or Silvani,
> masters of the forests, or Nymphs, but ceremonies of the gods
> barbarous in ritual, altars furnished with hideous offerings,
> and every tree is sanctified with human blood.
> If antiquity at all deserves credence for its awe of the gods,
> the birds fear to sit upon those branches,
> the beasts fear to lie in those thickets; on those woods
> no wind has borne down or thunderbolts shot from black
> clouds; though the trees present their leaves to no breeze,
> they have a trembling of their own. Water pours
> from black springs and the grim and artless
> images of gods stand as shapeless fallen tree-trunks.

> The decay itself and pallor of the timber now rotting
> is astonishing; not so do people fear deities worshipped
> in ordinary forms: so much does ignorance of the gods
> they dread increase their terror.[26]

Lucan also alludes to the practice of human sacrifice among the Gauls: 'the people who with grim blood-offering placate Teutates the merciless and Esus dread with savage altars and the slab of Taranis …'. Even allowing for a measure of dramatic exaggeration and a tendency on the part of Classical writers to emphasize the barbaric otherness of the Celtic world, human sacrifice and carved wooden images are attested in the archaeological record. The mention of trees sanctified with human blood is intriguing and may imply that individual trees were the focus of particular rituals.

Lucan's *Civil War* was frequently copied in medieval times with scribes adding marginalia and interlinear glosses. In the Berne glosses, the *Commenta Bernensia* compiled around the 9th century, a scribe asserts that the bodies of men were suspended in these trees near Marseilles writing: *homo in arbore suspenditur usque donec per cruorem membra digesserit* [men were hung from trees and bloodily dismembered]. While there is no certainty, it has been assumed this additional detail came from another early source that has not survived.[27] There may have been ritual practices in which specific trees had a sacrificial role.

At around the same time however, in the last century BC, the native owner of the Port sword would have fully understood the very different import of the exotic Tree of Life symbol hammered on his sword blade. Whether the name Korisios is that of its owner or its maker, or even the name of the sword itself is not known, and the name may be either Celtic, Italic or Greek. What is certain, however, is that the weapon is a distinctive La Tène type found in Switzerland and southern Germany.[28]

The subject of the Tree of Life or World Tree is an exceptionally widespread one and, unsurprisingly, the subject of an enormous body of literature. Images are particularly common in the Mediterranean world and in the Near East as early as the 4th millennium BC and are to be found in later Jewish, Muslim, Buddhist art and in Christian imagery where it is often represented by the cross.[29] As various writers have stressed, the concept of the religious significance of trees is well represented in Indo-European cultures, in Mesopotamian, Indian, Greek, Germanic and Celtic mythology.[30]

The motif on the Port sword, the 'palm and ibex motif', was particularly common in the Near East and in the Mediterranean region in the later Bronze Age and continued into the Iron Age where it seems to have been especially popular in Cyprus.[31] As well as being an exotic mark of prestige, the design presumably had a symbolic value for the owner of the sword who in all probability was quite familiar with its cosmological significance. As Mircea Eliade has written 'the appearance of life is the central mystery of the world. Life comes from somewhere that is not this world and finally departs from here and goes to the beyond … man need only decipher what the cosmos says in its many modes of being, and he will understand the mystery of life. But one thing seems clear beyond doubt: that the cosmos is a living organism, which renews itself periodically. The mystery of the inexhaustible appearance of life is bound up with the rhythmical renewal of the cosmos. This is why the cosmos was imagined in the form of a gigantic tree; the mode of being of the cosmos and first of all its capacity for endless regeneration, are symbolically expressed by the life of the tree'.[32]

The tree is the link between the three cosmic levels: heaven, earth and the world below. It is a link that may also be conceived as a wooden pillar or stake or, in some cultures, even as a pillar stone forming the cosmic axis. As the *axis mundi,* it is the central metaphysical link between the human world and that of the gods, and the source of both knowledge and fertility. The equation of a tree with a post, stake or pillar is indicated in ancient Indian texts where an animal to be sacrificed is bound to a sacred stake known as the *yūpa* that was considered an alternative form of the Tree of Life. In Ireland, it is no surprise to find various early Christian saints connected to a special tree or *bile* but one reference is especially intriguing in this respect: a 17th century record describes a tree associated with Saint Colman Mac Duach, of Kilmacduagh, Co. Galway, which grew near the church there and was said to have been planted by the saint and to have miraculous powers. It was called 'Cuaille Mhic Duach', *cúaille* meaning stake or pole, and implying that a man-made object might be another manifestation of a *bile* or sacred tree.[33]

A classic example of a wooden post forming the *axis mundi* occurs at Navan Fort. Here a great oak pillar, felled around 95 BC, stood in the centre of a huge circular wooden shrine some 40 m in diameter and a wheel-shaped design was created in the summit of a cairn that was built to entomb the timber structure. The vertical timber, several metres high, was the focus of these radial lines and this combination of pillar surmounted by a solar wheel is a remarkable illustration of the link between solar symbolism and the *axis mundi*.[34] In an examination of the Navan evidence, the historian Charles Doherty has argued that Navan was an inauguration place associated with universal kingship.[35] In performing a horse sacrifice that was a version of the *asva-medha* (Chapter 3) an individual would become a 'world king'. The great central post was indeed an *axis mundi* because, as in Vedic India, such a king could only reside in the sacred centre. He was a wheel-turner, a *cakravartin* (*cakra*- meaning wheel) who promotes the welfare of his people and who like the sun protects and destroys. The final structure at Navan, the clay mound, formed the king's seat or *forrad*, like the mound of that name at Tara. This clay capping was placed on top of the radial lines in the summit of the cairn that had the great timber pillar as their focal point. This combination of pillar and wheel is a version of the *cakrastambha* or 'wheel-pillar', a carved pillar surmounted by a solar wheel (Fig. 6.4). It is a representation of the cosmic pillar, the mythical axis of the world, and is a remarkable illustration, at Navan, of an Indo-European concept found in the earliest Indian cosmogony and reflected in the *Rig Veda*.

This belief may have found expression in Iron Age England too. It is surely significant that both a tree trunk and a wooden wheel-shaped object (interpreted as a solar symbol) were deposited in a pit in a Romano-British settlement at Wavendon Gate in Milton Keynes (Bucks). Their relationship is unknown but the context was very probably a ritual one. Pottery sherds, an iron spearhead and other iron objects had also been placed in the pit which was dated to the 3rd century AD. The trunk, that of an ash tree, was a substantial piece, a

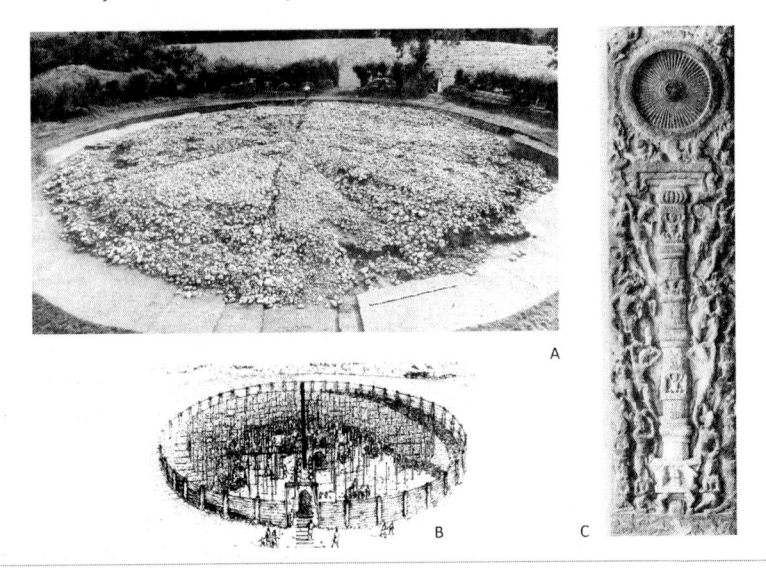

Figure 6.4. The axis mundi and the solar wheel. A. The radial divisions in the surface of the cairn at Navan (© Crown DfC). B. An artist's reconstruction of the building of the cairn in the 40m structure with the central pillar emphasized. C. A cakrastambha or wheel-pillar from Amaravati in the Government Museum Chennai, Madras.

section 1.35 m in length survived in the anaerobic conditions as did the greater part of the wheel-like object which had twelve spokes and a tenon (total length about 47 cm). It was made of oak and the tenon suggested it may once have been inserted in a timber post.[36]

While the cultic significance of timber uprights – at sanctuaries such as Aulnay-aux-Planches (Marne) and Libenice (Czech Republic) for instance – has been recognized for many years,[37] assigning cosmic significance to an individual timber post is not a task to be undertaken lightly but context may provide some support for such an interpretation. A large timber post that apparently stood before one of the Anglo-Saxon royal halls at Yeavering, Northumberland, may be one good example.[38] The same may be said of a timber post that stood on a central terrace (near the site of a three-pointed stone setting) in the major settlement at Helgö near Stockholm.[39]

6. *The Sacred Tree* 119

Though geographically far apart, two different Bronze Age examples of isolated timber pillars may also be mentioned to illustrate what may have been a widespread prehistoric phenomenon. The Navan pillar has been compared to the large pillar identified at the Goloring.[40] This huge circular earthwork near Koblenz in Germany was partially excavated in the 1940s. The monument is slightly smaller than Navan but is of similar bank and internal ditch construction. Activity there was dated to the late Bronze Age and possibly to the early Iron Age on the basis of a small quantity of pottery sherds and, given the absence of settlement evidence, it was assumed to be a ceremonial enclosure. The timber pillar that stood in its centre was estimated to have been 40–50 cm in diameter and 8–12 m high. The parallels between the Goloring and Navan are quite striking.

A timber pillar, set in a rock-cut pit over 1.20 m in depth, preceded the construction of a large oval enclosure containing Bronze Age cremated burials, deposits of charred grain and other features at Gransha, near Derry in the north of Ireland. The ditch of the enclosure had been deliberately diverted to cut through the post hole so the timber it had once contained must have been particularly significant.[41]

Though rare enough, images of what appear to be sacred trees (like the Port specimen) are a surer prospect when seeking such impressions of the supernatural in the archaeological record. A large leafy tree is depicted on one of the internal silver panels of the famous Gundestrup cauldron found in a Jutland bog in 1891. Dated to around 100 BC and of Celtic and Thracian inspiration, the fourteen plates of this unique object are decorated with a range of mythological images that have been the subject of extensive commentary. The scene in question represents a procession of armed warriors followed by three trumpet bearers approaching a giant figure on the left of the panel who is suspending a smaller figure over a vat or tub or ritual shaft (Fig. 6.5). A tree placed horizontally above these warriors has its roots near the vat and separates them from a group of mounted warriors above riding to the right.[42]

While the large standing figure is considered to be a deity, the panel as a whole has been interpreted in various ways: as a sacrificial ceremony involving the immersion an individual in a vessel in

Figure 6.5. Sketch of a panel on the Gundestrup cauldron, Jutland, depicting a procession of armed warriors and trumpet bearers approaching a figure who is suspending a smaller figure over a vat or ritual shaft. A tree with its roots exposed lies horizontally above the warriors.

an act of ritual drowning or, if the individual is being raised, a representation of the resurrection of a warrior from the dead. The scene has also been described as depicting an army on the march or a warrior initiation rite in which the lower group of individuals is transformed after immersion into mounted warriors, the leafy tree being a symbol of regeneration.[43] Vegetal motifs occur on a majority of the cauldron's panels but none of these leaves are the same as those on this singular object.[44] Even though it is even larger than the deity, the role of the sacred tree in the narrative is not clear. Whatever the explanation, it is a prominent motif and the details, from horses to weaponry, have prompted the suggestion that of all the Gundestrup panels, this 'is the only one of which the composition can with any confidence be claimed as Celtic'.[45] It is certainly a scene that demonstrates the importance of a whole tree in a complex ritual and it is noteworthy that it was not cut down but deliberately uprooted to expose its roots.

The model tree discovered in excavations in the Bavarian oppidum at Manching is a unique cult object. A wooden branch had been covered with sheet gold and had gold-covered bronze acorns and ivy leaves attached. This gold covered object, dated to about the 3rd century BC, is 72 cm in length and is an image of a living oak tree displaying a mixture of acorns and ivy leaves. Whether depicted as heart-shaped or trilobate, the leaves of the ever-green ivy had a symbolic significance in the Classical world being associated with various deities and this object has been considered a sacred device, perhaps a ritual processional staff carried by priest-like persons. Its divine associations give weight to the suggestion that the Gundestrup tree is also associated with a godlike figure and it too could be an oak entwined with ivy. In the Hellenistic world the symbolism of an ivy clad tree evoked the joining together of two persons, a metaphor that may well have found purchase in the Celtic world.[46] The Manching staff could conceivably have had a role in kingship ceremonial for it inevitably recalls the 'rod of kingship' of early Irish tradition. This was one of the elements in inauguration rituals that have parallels in the ancient Indo-European world [47] – and may echo prehistoric practices.

Whatever about kingly associations, the motif on the Port sword would suggest that there may be a connection between the image of the sacred tree and the ideology of a warrior caste. Ornate belt-hooks are clearly elite possessions being found in richly furnished Continental graves of late Hallstatt and early La Tène times where in many cases swords, belts and belt attachments are key elements of martial paraphernalia.[48] Decorative designs include geometrical and curvilinear motifs, vegetal motifs including leaf, palmette and lotus bud representations and animal, bird and human figures. Images of opposed fantastic beasts, the so-called griffin or 'dragon pairs', are a well-known protective emblem on swords and sword scabbards across much of the Celtic world from southern England to eastern Europe.[49] Just as opposed beasts offered protection to a sacred tree, presumably similar pairs of animals on sword or sword scabbard offered protection to the bearer of the weapon. Given the propensity for stylization in La Tène art, it should not be surprising to find the tree and animal motif appeared on weaponry in this guise as well. An animal pair flank a stylized tree on a scabbard from Bussy-le-Château (Marne), the tree being represented simply by a leaf-like motif (Fig. 6.6).

Opposed animals are also found on some belt-hooks flanking equally stylized tree-like motifs (Fig. 6.6). An example from a grave

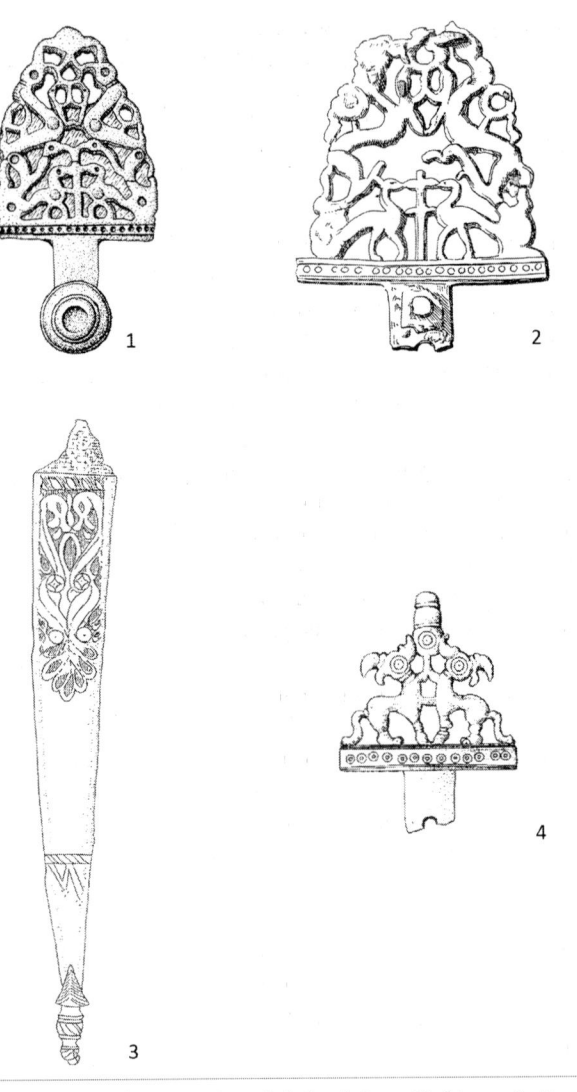

Figure 6.6. Stylized sacred trees. 1. On a belt-hook from Giubiasco, Switzerland. 2. On a belt-hook from Ensérune (Hérault), France. 3. An animal pair flank a stylized tree denoted by a leaf-like motif on a scabbard from Bussy-le-Château (Marne). 4. A stylized tree, or a pillar, with flanking animals is represented on a belt-hook from Somme-Bionne (Marne). Various scales.

in a cemetery near the oppidum of Ensérune in southern France depicts a pair of crudely delineated beasts facing a simplified and geometric tree with four branches. An analogous belt-hook from a grave at Giubiasco in Switzerland may come from the same workshop – and is just one of several with similar imagery.[50] A pair of fantastic animals face what may be a stylized tree, or a pillar, on a belt-hook from a famous chariot burial with rich grave goods at Somme-Bionne (Marne) dated to approximately 400 BC. Clearly a belief in the magical charge of such imagery preceded its appearance on the Port sword by several centuries and this particular use of tree and animal motifs was in all likelihood inspired by eastern Mediterranean fashion. However, its adoption was probably readily enabled because a belief in the sacred character of certain trees had much older and deeper roots in temperate Europe – as the Holme tree indicates.

CHAPTER 7

The Ancestors of Epona

The beautiful young woman who offered a golden cup and a great feast to Conn of the Hundred Battles and who was described as the eternal sovereignty of Ireland is the most striking image of the sovereignty goddess in Irish tradition. This supernatural figure's association with drinking ceremonial is apparent here and elsewhere. She is the personification of the land and inextricably linked to its fertility. Even so, this goddess is a fleeting figure in the mythological landscape, her different aspects manifested in a variety of different contexts. Her role in the sacred marriage that gave the right to rule to a prospective king was a mating ritual, a kingship wedding, that echoed an ancient belief that the female earth required male intervention to guarantee its fruitfulness. This union of immortal and mortal ensured the prosperity of the kingdom. In the associated rituals her earthly avatar was a mare, an aspect reflected in horse sacrifice and equine attributes. In some instances sovereignty has a war-like character too asserting authority through martial prowess.

The literary evidence is fragmentary of course and while it would be unwise to assume there was once a monolithic female deity embracing all these features, it is likely that the sovereignty goddess performed several functions. Even though some writers claim that some representations of the goddess Macha are late medieval creations, taken together they offer a good illustration of a memory of this multifunctionality.[1]

Macha is the sovereignty goddess associated with Navan Fort and she has several manifestations in medieval Irish literature. In one, she appears in the first version of *Cath Maige Tuired* (The Battle of Moytura) where she is described as a daughter of Ernmas of the Tuatha Dé Danann and is identified as one of the great war goddesses along with her sisters Badb and the Morrígan – whom we encountered at Oweynagat. It is said that Mag Macha – the plain of Macha around Navan Fort – was named after her and this is a situation in which such a goddess is also linked to the land as a sovereignty figure.

The *dindshenchas* tradition or lore of famous places, preserved in various medieval texts in prose and verse, is a rich mythological source that basically purports to explain how numerous places got their names. In the place-lore of the prose *Dindshenchas* of Ard Macha (the height of Macha: Armagh), we come across a second Macha who is the wife of Nemed, the leader of the third of the mythical invasions of Ireland in the *Lebor Gabála* (The Book of Invasions). She too is specifically associated with the plain of Macha, Mag Macha, and this is another instance in which a goddess has territorial associations. In another version of the *dindshenchas* tradition of Armagh, this Macha is credited with prophetic powers for she has a vision of the slaughter that will occur when the *Táin* is undertaken.

The third is a red-headed Macha, Macha Mongrúad, who is credited with creating the enclosure at Emain Macha in the metrical *Dindshenchas* description of that place. At one point this Macha disguises herself as a diseased person – a variant on the theme of the loathsome sovereignty figure whose beauty is restored with the appearance of a fitting ruler.[2] She appears as a martial figure repelling by force those who oppose her sovereignty in the prose *Dindshenchas*. Though puzzling to the modern reader, it is worth emphasizing that the generation of variants like this is a characteristic feature of myth where different accounts may confirm and complement rather than contradict one another.[3]

The best known of this quartet is Macha the wife of a man named Crunniuc. It is she who gave her name to Emain Macha when she gave birth to twins (*emain*). The second recension of *Noínden Ulad* (The Debility of the Ulstermen) gives the fullest account of this explanation for the name. It is exceptionally important in any consideration of the equine associations of the goddess and is worth quoting at length. This

Macha is represented as the supernatural wife of a wealthy mortal husband and their union evidently increased his wealth:[4]

> Crunniuc mac Agnomain of the Ulaid was a hosteller of one hundred cows. He lived in the wilderness and mountains and he had many sons. Moreover, his wife was dead. One day he was in his house on his own when he saw a woman coming towards him in the house. He deemed her appearance shapely. The woman immediately began to prepare food as if she were in a house she had always been in. When night came, she served the family without question. She slept with Crunniuc that night. She remained with them for a long time afterwards and they lacked no produce with her, neither food nor clothing nor wealth.
>
> It was not long after that that an assembly was held by the Ulaid. The Ulaid used to go to the assembly, both men and women, boys and girls. Moreover, Crunniuc went to the assembly along with everyone else. He was wearing good clothes and looking very prosperous. 'You are advised, then,' said the woman to him, 'not to say anything indiscreet.' 'That is unlikely,' he said.
>
> The assembly was gathered. The king's chariot was brought onto the green at the end of the day. The chariot and horses won. The crowd said, 'there is nothing faster than these horses.' Crunniuc said, 'my wife is faster.' He was immediately seized by the king. That is told to the woman. 'I am prevented from going to help him, however,' she said, 'for I am pregnant.' 'Although you may be hindered,' said the messenger, 'he will be killed unless you come.'
>
> She went to the assembly then and they got her a spancel. 'Help me,' she said to the crowd, 'for it was a mother who gave birth to each of you. Wait until I give birth.' They refused. 'Well then,' she said, 'there will be a greater evil because of it, and it will be upon the Ulaid for a long time.' 'What is your name?' said the king. She replied, 'my name and the name of my offspring will be given to this assembly forever. Macha daughter of Sainreth son of Imbath is my name'.

7. The Ancestors of Epona

Her highly ritualized actions in Crunniuc's dwelling are apparent in another version and present a picture of an Otherworld woman taking control of the domestic sphere and include her entering the house three times and twice turning *deiseal* or sunwise to enter the kitchen and to go to Crunniuc's bed.[5] His boastful utterance at the assembly or *óenach*, however, breaks his pledge of silence and discretion. His pregnant wife is forced to race, like a mare, against the horses of the king:

> She raced against the chariot then and when the chariot reached the end of the green her childbirth began in front of it. So that she gave birth to twins, a boy and a girl. It is from this that Emain Macha was named then. She cried out in her childbirth. Anyone who heard her fell ill for five days and four nights. That pain used to come perpetually to every Ulsterman who was there, for nine generations of each man who was there. Five days and four nights, or five nights and four days. That was the affliction of the Ulaid. Each of the Ulstermen had the strength of a woman in childbirth for nine generations during the affliction. Three people among the Ulaid who did not suffer the affliction: boys, the women of the Ulaid, and Cú Chulainn. This is the period it remained on the Ulstermen: from the time of Crunniuc mac Agnomain meic Curir Ulad meic Fiatach meic Urmi to the time of Forc mac Dallain meic Mainich meic Lugdach *etc*. The Ulaid are named after Curir Ulad. This, then, is the cause of the affliction of the Ulaid and the origin of the name Emain Macha.

She gives birth to twins and curses the Ulstermen who for nine generations must suffer the same debility as she, a weakness that means that only Cú Chulainn can defend Ulster when Medb and the men of Connacht attack as recounted in the *Táin*.

The unusual equine dimension to this tale is highly significant.[6] It probably echoes a memory of horse rituals linked to kingship ceremonial at prehistoric Navan akin to that inauguration rite and horse sacrifice of the Cenél Conaill in Donegal described in Chapter 3. Macha, it seems, was a horse goddess and sovereignty figure, a mare being her earthly surrogate. She is, by the way, not the only figure with equine links associated with Navan. A certain Echaid or Eochaid who was said to have held the kingship of Emain for nineteen years had a supernatural horse, the tallest in Ireland. On one occasion when it urinated, the force of its waters created a deep well in the ground that eventually erupted to produce Lough Neagh – 'The lake of Echaid'.[7]

Many writers have considered the peculiar role of horses in the episode in the story The Debility of the Ulstermen as an important detail reflecting not just Macha's equine nature but also linking her to the Welsh goddess Rhiannon. The latter figures in the series of medieval prose tales known as the Mabinogion and her name derives from *Rigantona, 'Great Queen'.[8] In one story she appears as an Otherworld figure riding a great white horse and is pursued by Pwyll, Lord of Dyfed. Her horse is magical and he is never able to catch up with her. She eventually halts and indicates that she wishes to be his bride but tricked into keeping a careless promise, Pwyll is obliged to permit her betrothal to a certain Gwawl who in turn is outwitted and induced to relinquish his claim. After some time the union of Pwyll and Rhiannon produces a male child but on the night of his birth the boy disappears. Accused of infanticide, she is sentenced to spend seven years at the mounting block outside the gate of the court and to offer to carry strangers to the court on her back like a horse. Teyrnon Twrf Liant, Lord of Gwent, has a mare that foaled with great regularity every May day and each foal would promptly disappear. On this occasion, coinciding with the boy's birth, he prevented a fine newly-born colt from being stolen and simultaneously found a child at the door. After four years the colt is given to the child who has grown prodigiously. Teyrnon then recognizes the boy as the son of Pwyll and takes him to the court where Rhiannon is released from her punishment.

Like Macha, Rhiannon has been seen as a goddess of sovereignty: she possesses the principal features of this figure who seeks and promotes an acceptable male candidate for kingship. She deliberately chooses Pwyll as her mate, offers him a feast, he achieves wisdom, consummates his marriage and after various difficulties, he has a son and secures dynastic succession.[9] In addition, the other threads of evidence that connect the stories of Macha, wife of Crunniuc, and Rhiannon are noteworthy. In each there is a horse race with supernatural qualities. There is a contest between a goddess and a king. A birth follows: twins in the case of Macha, the simultaneous birth of Pryderi and a colt in the case of Rhiannon. Both are compromised by the careless comments of their respective mates and, most significantly, both undergo a humiliation that blurs the distinction between horse and woman. It is an interesting possibility that this mythical melding of woman and horse is represented in some of those images of horses with human heads on Gaulish coins (Fig. 7.2, 4).

The birth of twins in each tale is a significant detail for there are echoes of other older mythic themes here. Mythological twins are widely represented in Indo-European tradition where they are regularly associated with horses or in some cases represented as horses. The Greek Castor and Pollux (the Dioscuri), the Roman Romulus and Remus and possibly the Anglo-Saxon Hengist and Horsa are perhaps the best known.[10]

The equine and female dimension has suggested a connection between both Macha and Rhiannon and the horse goddess Epona. Indeed it is now almost a century since the French scholar Henri Hubert first identified Rhiannon as a supernatural figure with equine qualities that recalled Epona.[11] Several decades later, Jean Gricourt and Georges Dumézil simultaneously and independently noted the comparable association of Macha with horses and recognized the now familiar equine links between Epona, Rhiannon and Macha.[12]

Epona is well known in several hundred carvings and inscriptions in the Gallo-Roman world notably in eastern Gaul and in the Rhineland. Her Celtic origin is clear, her Celtic name deriving from Indo-European *ekwos (horse) like the Old Irish *ech*. In the Roman world she is invariably depicted with one or more horses, sometimes with a mare and a foal or seated side-saddle on a mare or between two horses or donkeys. She is also often shown carrying a variety of items, most commonly a dish full of fruit or a cornucopia (a horn of plenty – a symbol of abundance). As Miranda Green has indicated she was a complex figure with a set of roles and functions that ranged from that of benefactress and dispenser of life's bounties – in fact a form of mother-goddess – to presider over healing thermal sanctuaries and over the dead in their tombs.[13] While mostly venerated as a domestic goddess who was a protector of horses, her original Celtic form may have been one of higher status perhaps combining features of war goddess and sovereignty figure as in the several manifestations of Macha. The equine features that link Macha and Rhiannon may be the remnants of an ancient mythology that once associated a pre-Roman ancestor of Epona with equine and kingship rituals.

Given the great gulf between medieval text and Gallo-Roman times and the different functions of the figures of Macha and Rhiannon compared to Epona, it is unsurprising that there are those who consider any attempt to link them as methodologically questionable,[14] but it is possible to present a good case in support of the argument that figures like Macha and Rhiannon may have been older and more powerful precursors of Epona in prehistoric Europe.

Just such an equine deity is discernible in south-western Iberia in the mid- 1st millennium BC. An early script called Tartessian, named after the semi-historical Tartessos somewhere near the mouth of the Guadalquivir River, is dated to approximately 650–400 BC and contains some Celtic names and linguistic forms. An important and intriguing inscription is recorded in southern Portugal (Fig. 7.1). A funerary slab, found at Benaciate, San Bartolomeu de Messines, Faro, bears an almost complete dedication that reads in translation: 'For the ones whom I [this grave] carry, for Asuna, the supreme one, for Ekurini ... deliverance [literally running under]'. According to John Koch the name Ekurini combines the elements *ekwos and *rīgnī 'queen' and is an early reference to a 'horse queen' akin to Macha and Rhiannon. Asuna survives as a female name in Gaul.

A second slab from this site, of similar size, has the remnants of an inscription and a low-relief carving of a helmeted woman riding side-saddle on a horse and holding what may be a cornucopia in her left hand, a pose recalling some images of Epona who is sometimes invoked as Eponae Reginae 'to queen Epona'.[15] The helmet, if such it is,

7. *The Ancestors of Epona* 131

Figure 7.1. The Ekurini inscription. Written in Tartessian c. 500 BC in southern Portugal, the name refers to a 'horse queen'.

might be an allusion to the figure's martial qualities. The importance of the Ekurini inscription lies in the fact that it reveals the presence of a mythical equine figure in this part of Europe at the dawn of history.

Traces of mythic equine figures are apparent elsewhere too. In eastern Europe, a legend of the Székelys, a Hungarian people in what is now Romania, declares they are all brothers because they are the descendants of a white mare. There is a story associated with a lake associated with a local St Anna that involves a chariot race between two lords to decide the right of possession of a property. This involves the humiliating harnessing of a girl named Anna to a chariot like a horse. She curses both the man in question and the countryside, upon which he and his fortress disappear and the lake is born. She then builds a chapel and lives there. This may be a Christianized version of a myth analogous to that of Rhiannon and Macha.[16]

There is a strange tale in the 13th century Icelandic *Landnámabók* (Book of Settlements) in which a man named Thorir Dúfunef acquires an exceptionally fast mare named Fluga who comes from abroad in a ship with a cargo of livestock. A magician named Örn challenges him to a horse-race that was won by Fluga who proved to be twice as fast as her challenger. A disappointed Örn retreates to a mountain then called Arnarfell (the mountain of Örn) and kills himself. The exhausted Fluga is left alone while Thorir attended the Althing (assembly). On his return he finds that there was a grey stallion with a black mane with his mare who then gives birth to a foal. From this line comes a horse named Eidfaxi who kills seven men in one day before being killed himself. Fluga loses her life in a swamp at a place then called Flugumyri.

Like many a tale in the Irish *dindshenchas* tradition, on one level this is a story that explains the names of various places (Arnarfell and Flugumyri for instance). Because there are references elsewhere in the sagas to the drowning of a horse and a bull in bogs, possibly as sacrifices to the god Freyr, it has been suggested that the puzzling death of the mare Fluga, abruptly described in a short sentence, was also a horse sacrifice. The supernatural elements in the story, the appearance of the sorcerer Örn and his death implying that the magical horse-race may really have been a contest between life and death, a strangely coloured stallion (perhaps Freyr himself) who mates with the mare, and the birth of a foal eventually producing the murderous Eidfaxi, all combine to suggest that Fluga was no ordinary horse.[17]

The sacral role of the horse is an ancient one. It is evident on the famous Trundholm chariot *c.* 1500 BC and in later Bronze Age imagery on rock art and on metalwork in Scandinavia (Chapter 5). The horse's function in transporting the sun across the heavens and then through an underworld to its rebirth in the east is an immensely significant cosmic task. Yet, surprisingly, it is a role supplanted by magical birds in the later Bronze Age with the appearance of the image of the solar boat with bird's head prow and stern. At some time in the Bronze Age, perhaps around the middle of the 2nd millennium, the role of the horse begins to undergo a fundamental change. The depiction of an image of a human figure riding a horse-drawn two-wheeled chariot on one of the Kivik pictorial stones and the appearance of wheeled vehicles, pulled by horses, in Scandinavian rock art and on Iberian stelae, all suggest a new ceremonial role for the animal.[18] It is a role linked to an elite stratum of society, presumably male and at times identifiable as a warrior caste.

It is remarkable that horses play such a strange role in the medieval stories of both Macha and Rhiannon and it is even stranger that both women are forced to effectively become horse-like. This mythic union is dramatically illustrated on an unprovenanced Iron Age coin perhaps from Brittany bearing a winged mare with a human head, seven udders and what appears to be a sleeping foal below (Fig. 7.2, 4). The presence of multiple udders implies fertility, and the presence of a foal here and on other coins, like the example from the Mans region (Pays de la Loire) with a mare, a monstrous creature above and a suckling foal below, recalls some representations of Epona that emphasize her nurturing aspects. As already mentioned, in Gallo-Roman iconography she is a much reduced entity deprived of any war-like attributes, displaying protective and caring qualities.

Images of naked and armed women riding horses on coins may be representations of war goddesses and the suggestion these may be allusions to mythic themes associated with another aspect of the predecessor of that Gallo-Roman Epona is entirely reasonable.[19] On one of these, a coin of the Redones from the Rennes region the woman is depicted holding a shield in her right hand and a dagger in her left (Fig. 7.2, 2). This reversal is presumably an allusion to the woman's Otherworldly nature (Chapter 5). Depictions of shrines or temples associated with or even containing a horse are known on a number of Gaulish coins.[20] These could be shrines to a horse goddess.

134 *Myth and Materiality*

Figure 7.2. 1–2. Coins of the Redones from the Rennes area depicting an armed and naked female figure astride a horse. 3. Coin of the Aulerci Cenomani from the Mans region (Pays de la Loire) with a mare, a (marine?) monster above and a suckling foal below. 4. Unprovenanced coin perhaps from Brittany bearing a winged mare with a human head, seven udders and a (sleeping?) foal below. 5. Image of a shrine or temple and a horse on a coin of the Eburovici.

Other female figures had equine links too. Macha may not have been alone in early Ireland for there are a few scraps of evidence to suggest that this may have been the case with Medb of Rathcroghan. Her lover Fergus was known as Ro-ech, 'Great Horse', and the name of one of her several husbands Eochaid may be connected with Old Irish *ech*, 'horse'.[21] To this may be added the statement by Fergus comparing her leadership of the army in the *Táin* to a herd of horses led by a mare. There is also the odd episode when Medb passes water and thereby creates three great trenches that recalls the capacity of a horse to produce a remarkable amount of urine in one go – a landscape-altering event that recalls the well created by Eochaid's supernatural horse.

There is also the significant reference in the *dindshenchas* of Fert Medba (Medb's Grave) that refers to her ability to outrun the swiftest horses: in the translation by Edward Gwynn – 'there was a day when horses would not be loosed against the daughter of Eochaid *feidlech*'.[22] It is interesting to note that one of the two great British queens recorded in Classical sources has equine associations as well. Clearly the meaning of a horse epithet applied to a historical personage is difficult to gauge but maybe it had some supernatural connotation that conferred a special status: the name of Cartimandua of the Brigantes may mean well-groomed or sleek pony.[23]

In seeing the various representations of Macha as war goddess and sovereignty goddess, we have dual aspects of the same entity who also has equine characteristics. Horse goddess, sovereignty goddess, kingship rituals and horse sacrifice are inextricably linked. When those earlier writers, Hubert, Gricourt and Dumézil, addressed the links between Macha, Rhiannon and Epona there was very limited evidence for horse ritual of any sort in prehistoric Ireland, Britain or Continental Europe. In recent decades the picture has changed almost beyond recognition. The evidence we now have for the cultic importance of the horse and for horse sacrifice suggest widespread ritual practices conceivably associated with the mythic ancestors of Epona.

While the slaughter of small furry creatures may have been ritually important, oxen and horses were valuable animals unlikely

Figure 7.3. An artist's sketch of a horse burial found in an enclosure ditch in an Iron Age settlement at Cagny (Normandy).

to be casually disposed of. Their sacrifice would have been especially rich in symbolism. Indeed, at times horse sacrifice may have been a particularly tumultuous, violent and spectacular ritual drama. The anodyne drawings of buried horses that figure from time to time in archaeological reports give few clues as to what may have actually transpired (Fig. 7.3). In the Hindu sacrifice, the horse was suffocated (Chapter 3) to avoid the shedding of blood and perhaps horse sacrifice was intended to be as non-violent as possible. Careful blood letting may have been practised on occasion. At times, however, sacred violence may have been customary as with the pole-axing of ten stallions at Vertault, Côte d'Or (Fig. 7.4). Fear in horses is contagious and multiple killings of this sort, or even of just pairs of horses, must have been particularly strident and savage events.

Radiocarbon dating of some horse teeth found with other horse bones in front of the great passage tomb at Newgrange has demonstrated that they actually date to the first two centuries AD.[24] This raises the intriguing possibility that horse sacrifice may have been a dramatic and theatrical part of the Roman-period offerings of gold coins and other objects deposited before that monument. These may have been offerings to one of the gods of Newgrange, that Nuadu of the silver hand of the Tuatha Dé Danann who is cognate with the Romano-British Nodens.[25]

Figure 7.4. Plan of the great pit at Vertault (Côte d'Or) containing ten sacrificed stallions.

One other Irish discovery is also very significant. In 1903 a small tumulus was investigated in the townland of Farta, Co Galway (the name being an anglicization of the Irish *fert*, burial mound).[26] It measured 12 m in diameter and 2.7 m in height and stood just 500 m from the celebrated Turoe Stone. A Bronze Age cordoned urn burial and cremation, possibly dating to about 1500 BC, was found on a slab on the ground surface at the mound's centre. Over a thousand years later the extended body of a woman aged between 20–25 years was inserted into the older monument. She was accompanied by some pieces of antler and a small horse (a seven year old stallion) laid on its left side. Strontium and oxygen isotope analysis suggests the woman was not of local origin but spent her formative years in eastern Ireland or eastern England. Interestingly, she had an inward twisting of the knee or in-toeing and this would have given her an abnormal gait. This physical impairment may have conferred her with a special status like the women of Vix and Juellinge.

This female burial was radiocarbon dated to cal AD 383–536, the horse to cal AD 388–536 (calibrated at 2 sigma) and they are thus contemporary interments as the excavator thought. We do not know how the horse died but since it and the woman are unlikely to have expired simultaneously, horse sacrifice is a distinct possibility. It is interesting that this woman, buried with a horse but without any other prestigious goods, may have been just as important in her own community in the west of Ireland as the 'princess of Vix' in eastern France centuries before.

The deer antler remains, which were stated to be 'by the side of the human skeleton on the south side', were dated to cal AD 564–677 and were presumably introduced into the burial one if not two centuries later when the significance of woman and horse was evidently still remembered.[27] It does seem likely that residual pagan belief in the sacral significance of the horse survived well into the medieval period in Ireland.

Though rare enough, Iron Age horse and human burials are known elsewhere. The presence of a horse or the commoner occurrence of horse equipment, wagon or chariot fitments, are generally interpreted as the inclusion of prestige elements in the funerary sphere as an expression of the elite status of the individual interred. Thus the early 19th century discovery of a pair of horses, chariot parts and a human skeleton beneath a barrow at Arras in Yorkshire was labelled 'The King's Barrow' because of its apparent importance.[28] Poorly recorded Iron Age finds of humans and horses are known from Mildenhall, Suffolk, and Fordington, Dorset.[29] Once again, horse sacrifice is a probability since animal and deceased are unlikely to have died at the same time.

Across the Channel in Normandy, a chariot burial and a pair of horses were found at Orval (Manche). A pit with a wooden chamber within a small rectangular ditched enclosure was found to contain parts of a two-wheeled chariot including finely decorated linchpins, remains of two horses, harness fitments, a spear and sword. The human remains, presumably male, did not survive acidic soil conditions.[30] Another find is recorded from Nanterre in western Paris: horse bones, iron weaponry and chariot fitments were recovered over century ago but no details are preserved.[31] An exceptional chariot burial was discovered at Warcq near Charleville-Mézières in the Ardennes in

7. The Ancestors of Epona

2014. Along with sword and rich grave goods, the body, presumably male, had been placed on the vehicle and was accompanied by four horse, two in front of the chariot and two in opposite corners of the grave.[32] Since all four animals are unlikely to have died together, horse sacrifice seems a certainty. This and the rarity of finds like these is probably a good indication of their special nature.

Beyond the Iron Age funerary sphere, in England, the great white horse carved in the chalk on the Berkshire Downs at Uffington was created a number of centuries before or after 1000 BC and seems to have been reworked and maintained over the millennia thereafter. It is an important indication of the ritual importance of the horse in Britain at an early date. It has been considered a tribal symbol but it may once have had a role in rituals of kingship.[33] Since kingship and solar symbolism are connected in Irish tradition, the white horse may well have been an element in that Bronze Age solar cosmology in which mythical horses were believed to guide the course of the sun.[34]

There is no shortage of evidence for the cultic significance of the horse from various parts of the Celtic-speaking world in later prehistory. In England, an important early find comes from Runnymede, Berkshire, where a large pit on the periphery of a late Bronze Age settlement by the Thames contained the dismembered bones of a stallion. Its forelimbs were in articulation and deliberately crossed one over the other. This had to be done deliberately because it is a position a horse is incapable of adopting in life and not easily employed in death either. The remains had been placed in a large pit that had held a timber post that may have been removed before the deposition of the horse bones around 1000 BC. The fill of the pit contained the remains of a hearth that seemed to have been inverted when placed in the pit – with well-fired clay lying on top of charcoal. This appeared to be an act to formally seal the horse remains below. Pottery sherds were found beside and beneath the hearth and other finds from the upper fill included an antler cheek piece, an antler tine, a loom-weight and a fragment of a bronze socketed knife. These and some adjacent stake holes were among the details that suggested that the horse remains were the subject of continued veneration for some time.[35]

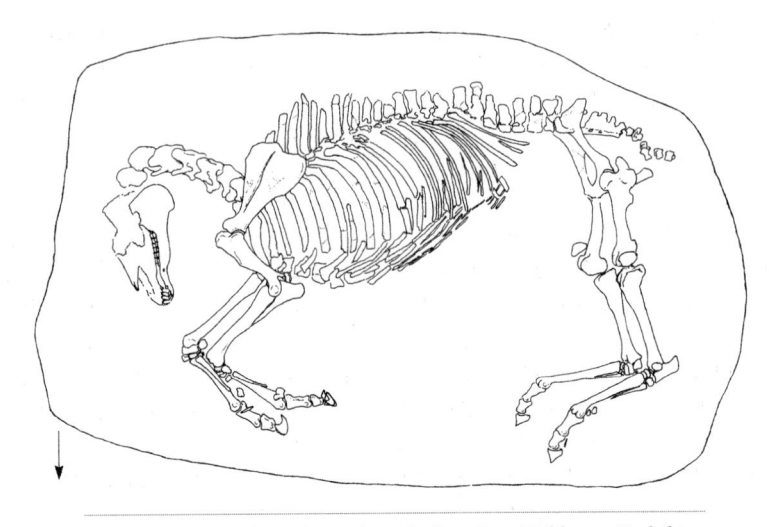

Figure 7.5. One of two horse burials found at Kirkburn, Yorkshire.

Two horse burials were found at Kirkburn, Yorkshire, in an Iron Age cemetery of the Arras Tradition. The horses were buried in separate pits in shallow ring ditches near an undated square enclosure; they were similarly orientated east–west, lying on their right side with head to the east. They were radiocarbon dated to the late 1st or early 2nd century AD, several centuries later than nearby burials (Fig. 7.5).[36] A pair of horse burials was found in front of a Romano-British settlement at Barton Field, Tarrant Hinton, Dorset. Both animals were complete, placed in separate shallow pits, laid on their left sides with heads towards the north. Some pottery sherds indicated a 4th century date.[37] It does seem that the burial of pairs of horses had some special significance.

At Mill Hill, near Deal, in Kent, two cemeteries of Iron Age burials were found. They consisted for the most part of simple pits containing unburnt skeletons, a few with grave goods such as brooches of the mid-2nd to mid-1st centuries BC. The largest burial group also contained a horse burial, the complete skeleton of a six to seven year old mare. This burial was found some 50 m to the north of that exceptional male burial with bronze crown accompanied by a shield, an iron sword in a decorated bronze scabbard and other grave goods (Fig. 4.3).

The excavations at the hillfort of Danebury, Hampshire, revealed that all the domestic animals found at the site – including sheep, cattle, pigs, dogs and horses – were also represented in special propitiatory offerings deposited in disused storage pits.[38] A disproportionately high number of horse skulls had been deposited in pits as well. Some horse remains were evidently especially important: one pit contained a horse skeleton associated with approximately 50 sling stones, some chalk blocks and a dog skeleton; the horse's head had been deliberately removed and placed next to the dog. Indeed even among the randomly distributed bones in Danebury it was clear that horse and dog bones were more frequently found together in the same archaeological context than might be expected given their relative scarcity in the animal bone assemblage generally.[39]

A crouched burial in a small cemetery of 4th–3rd century BC date at Cliffs End, Isle of Thanet, Kent, consisted of the remains of a subadult, probably male, placed on top of the partial remains of a horse. This male animal may have been partly dismembered. An associated bone group found 3 m to the east was comprised of some bones of a male dog and their partial nature (skull, hind paws, one front paw and tail) suggested the deposition of a dog pelt rather than a complete skeleton.[40] Interestingly, the deposition of horse pelts has been recorded in France: at Neuville-aux-Bois (Loiret) the lower fill of an Iron Age storage pit contained the four lower limbs of a horse, a neck bone and tail bones deposited in such a way as to suggest a pelt folded over on itself. In the same general region a storage pit at Prasville (Eure-et-Loir) produced a similar assemblage comprising four lower limbs and some tail bones.[41]

An exceptional discovery comes from Blewburton, Oxfordshire (Fig. 7.6). Excavations in the late 1940s uncovered the burial of a human skeleton, a horse and a dog in the lower levels of the ditch of a hillfort some 8 m north of the entrance.[42] While some displacement of the bones had occurred, it did appear that the horse was laid on its left side and the human was positioned with one leg over and the other

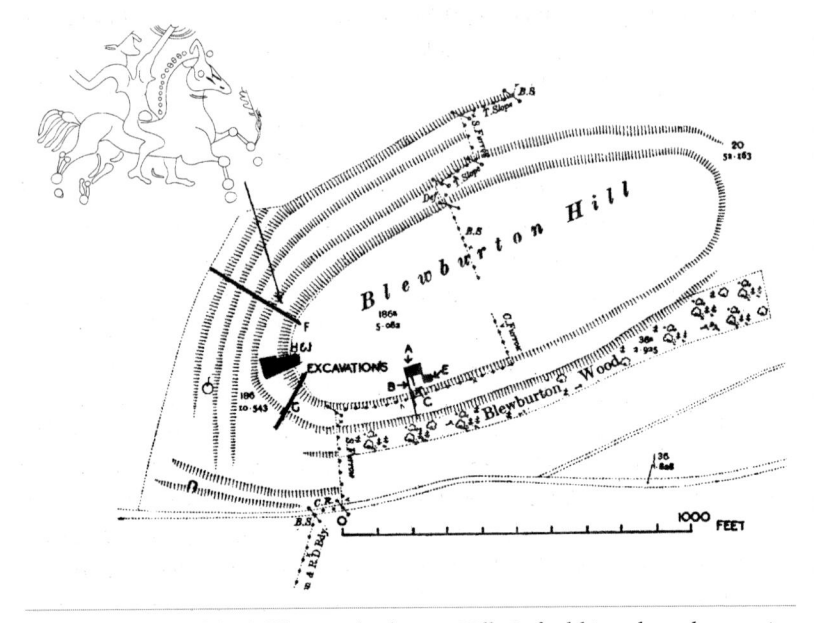

Figure 7.6. Plan of the hillfort at Blewburton Hill, Oxfordshire where the remains of a woman placed astride a horse were found in cutting F in the ditch north of the entrance. The image on the top left is that on a Breton coin illustrated in Figure 7.2.

leg under the horse's hindquarters with the complete skeleton of a dog below. Associated finds included an iron adze, a burnished black pottery vessel, and numerous quartzite pebbles. In a careful re-evaluation of this find Robin Bendrey and others have demonstrated that two individuals are represented in the human skeletal assemblage, one denoted by a femur, the other (thought originally to be a male straddling the horse) is probably a tall female. The horse is female, the dog male. This deliberate configuration of a woman astride a mare, placed in the base of a hillfort ditch, must have had some special symbolic import.[43]

It recalls the images of naked horse-riding women on some Gaulish coins, conceivably war goddesses, already mentioned (Fig. 7.2, 1–2). Placed on the perimeter of a settlement, like the horse burial at Runnymede, it may have had some protective significance. The animal skulls found in the upper levels of a ditch on the northern outskirts of Battlesbury Camp, a hillfort in Wiltshire, may have had a similar purpose. Three horse skulls and seven cattle skulls had been carefully prepared (with the removal of tissue and bone) probably for display on timber posts.[44] This may have been a widespread custom, for at the famous site of La Tène in Switzerland for instance weaponry and horses' heads seem to have been displayed as trophies and some horse skulls there exhibited traces of having been fixed on spikes.[45]

The curious and repetitive commingling of horse remains and other animal bones occurs elsewhere and such purposeful action again suggests more than the casual disposal of animal waste. At Winterborne Kingston, Dorset, several pits in an Iron Age enclosure contained the disarticulated remains of cattle and horse in which composite animals had been created from the deliberate reassembly of cow and horse bone. In one, the articulated skeleton of an adult male, dated to the early 1st century BC, was found lying face down over a major deposit of disarticulated cow and horse bone.[46] A similarly complex Iron Age rite has been recorded at Varennes-sur-Seine (Seine-et-Marne), south-east of Paris, where a large deep pit contained the skeleton of an adolescent covered in turn by a deposit of bones of a dog and four horses, a layer of sand and then a further deposit of bones of three horses and a dog.[47]

In northern France, horse remains were a relatively minor component among the animals sacrificed at the sanctuary at Gournay-sur-Aronde where cattle, sheep and pig predominated and horse bones formed a part of the great ossuary at Ribemont-sur-Ancre east of Amiens.[48] However, of the many other discoveries of horse remains in late prehistoric Continental cult sites those at Vertault (Côte d'Or) and Gondole (Puy-de-Dôme) are surely among the most extraordinary. The site of a small Gallo-Roman temple at Vertault was the focus for the earlier deposition in the 1st century AD of the remains of some 200 dogs, 42 horses and a few sheep and cattle. All males, horses were buried with heads to the south, dogs with heads to the west and they were placed in pits of varying sizes. One large pit contained the carcasses of ten poleaxed stallions all lying on their right side on a north–south axis (Fig. 7.4). Significantly, 10 pits in the immediate vicinity contained the skeletons of 17 dogs.[49] Near the oppidum of Gondole, south-east of Clermont-Ferrand in the Auvergne, an area devoted to animal burial in pits, notably horses, included one large rectangular pit containing the skeletons of seven adults, one child and eight horses.[50]

Another discovery in Clermont-Ferrand at Le Brézet consisted of the complete and articulated skeleton of a horse placed in a deep pit. Traces of a small rectangular box were found beneath it between its fore and hind limbs and this had contained elements of iron horse harness and a bronze torc. Pottery sherds and a glass bead were also a part of the deposit.[51]

Two simpler horse burials found at Cagny, east of Caen in Normandy, may seem to be less impressive deposits but may have been of major ritual significance nonetheless. One was placed in the upper fill of the ditch of a rectangular enclosure in an extensive Iron Age settlement dating to around 500 BC (Fig. 7.3). A four year old stallion had been buried some 12 m from the enclosure entrance possibly as a rite linked to the abandonment of this particular habitation site or even as a foundation deposit for a new adjacent one. A second horse had been buried in a linear ditch that intersected with another rectangular enclosure but it was less well preserved. It had been placed in the bottom of the ditch at a point deliberately enlarged to contain it and before the ditch began to silt up naturally. The remains of the young stallion displayed no signs of butchery and the animal was assumed to have died a natural death but of course suffocation and blood letting are just two ways of killing that might leave no trace. The fact that these two animals were the only ones deposited in a complete state does suggest they had some special significance.[52]

Diverse and geographically scattered as they are, these symbolically charged activities do illustrate the unusual importance of the horse in ritual contexts in late prehistoric times. The high status of the horse throughout the Celtic world is well documented.[53] The deposition of horse trappings in graves is one example of this of course, but the presence of this sort of material in female burials, including their use as items of personal adornment (such as a horse bit used as a composite neck ornament in a Hallstatt grave) raises interesting questions about their symbolic significance in such a context given the links between horses and powerful mythological women.[54]

The horse's extra-mundane qualities are illustrated in other diverse ways – notably by depiction of a winged animal. This supernatural aspect finds its most extensive expression in the iconography of silver and gold Romano-British and Gaulish coinage. John Creighton has clearly demonstrated that the horse along with a male head on the obverse is a persistent and dominant image on British gold coins. He suggests this recurrent pairing could symbolize the sacred marriage fundamental to sacral authority.[55] That the equine image may have a supernatural significance is indicated time and again. Associated minor symbols such as crescent shapes, dots and circular motifs, all raise a host of questions – especially since these motifs are all but absent from the repertoire of contemporary metalwork. In any event, since bird imagery is inextricably linked with the concept of the Otherworld in both early Irish literature and archaeological iconography, the presence of wings undoubtedly points to the animal's Otherworldly nature. Shamanic practice might be encoded in images of winged horses too (Fig. 7.2, 4) for in many traditional societies flight is the shaman's route to the spirit-world.[56] Such images are not simple copies of the figure of Pegasus (very rare on Roman coinage) and the indigenous development of a horse with wings did not require a Classical prototype.[57]

The ritual importance of the horse over a wide area of Iron Age Europe is not in doubt and only a fraction of the evidence is noted here. Horse sacrifice, in all its various forms, obviously does not prove the existence of a horse goddess. It had a most serious purpose of course and the burial of the remains of a valuable animal in the earth was probably a propitiatory offering of some description. To see it as an expression of hope for prosperity and peace is not unreasonable. Since a female sovereignty figure represented the fertility of the land in Irish tradition, such a mythical personage – an ancestor of Epona – could well have been the intended recipient.

That myths reflecting this sacral dimension should survive into early medieval times in Ireland is more difficult to demonstrate but clearly this question is of fundamental importance in any consideration of the possible prehistoric origins of Macha's equine character. The activity at Farta involving the deposition of antler indicates that the importance of that particular horse burial was still remembered in the 7th century AD several centuries after the introduction of Christianity. The process of Christianization in Ireland is often depicted as a tale of triumphal progress in which, by the 7th century, Ireland was formally Christian. In a process of religious syncretism, the new religion triumphed over paganism and there is no denying its dominant position at an elite level in society where, at times, it seems to have been enthusiastically and peacefully embraced. That said, there is good evidence that pagan traditions persisted long after the introduction of Christianity.

Today with a truly impressive body of evidence to hand for the ritual importance of the horse in the Celtic world and a greater appreciation of the long persistence of pagan beliefs in Ireland, we can be more confident that medieval texts provide a glimpse of a much older powerful sovereignty figure with equine attributes. Macha and Rhiannon – and others whose names are lost to us – may each have been just one of a number of ancient realizations of a single powerful supernatural concept. Epona became their revered but diminished descendant.

Epilogue

Traces of the mythological forebears of Epona are to be found in both medieval texts and in the archaeological record where that reference to Ekurini from San Bartolomeu de Messines tells us the 'horse queen' already had a mythological presence around 500 BC. Medieval literature preserves no more than fragments of a mythic structure that once melded horse and woman in the form of a horse goddess who represented the land itself. This sovereignty figure played a fundamental role in the rituals of sacral kingship. As the Scandinavian evidence demonstrates, the cultic importance of the horse is as old as the Bronze Age, probably predating the famous Trundholm chariot of the sun to at least 1500 BC. It would seem to be one of the many aspects of an Indo-European tradition that has left its own mark in later mythologies in Ireland and Continental Europe.

As horse and wagon and other related objects became symbols of an elite stratum of society, bird imagery replaced the horse as an accompaniment to solar symbols but not, it seems, supplanting the horse's Otherworldly associations. This is reflected in the emergence of the practice of horse sacrifice that, from Runnymede to Vertault, has many different forms. There was undoubtedly a complex belief system behind these practices. Protective magic, warrior ideology and elite symbolism may all have had a role to play at different times. A constant, however, is the deposition of horse remains in the earth. This was probably a reaffirmation of that animal's special link with the land and its fertility, and with the goddess who represented this concept.

According to Irish tradition this goddess had associations with martial violence as well. This is a link that is graphically depicted on those Gaulish coins with images of naked and armed horse-riding women. It also is a theme that is surely expressed in the burial of horse and woman at Blewburton Hill but an aspect that no longer survives in the depictions of Epona in the Romanised world.

A striking feature of this material is the fact that the archaeological evidence comes from different periods and from widely different places. Those who seek a neat pattern of continuity in any part of Europe at any time will be disappointed. The dispersed nature of the evidence, however, may actually tell a different story. Equine imagery on stone is virtually confined to Bronze Age Scandinavia and Iberia but the horse was known throughout Europe at this time and yet only found graphic expression in these two particular regions. This tells us something important about the partiality of the archaeological record. A widely scattered distribution pattern, with many empty spaces, may in reality represent an equally widespread presence.

There may have been a universal notion of a reversed or inverted Otherworld as well but, bearing in mind the bias of the funerary record, it should be no surprise to find that this belief is only discernible here and there in prehistoric Europe. The same may be said of those images of inverted or reversed solar boats that represent the nocturnal voyage of the sun through the Otherworld in such different times and places as Scandinavia and Central Europe in the Bronze Age and Ireland and Britain in the later Iron Age. The nocturnal voyage of the sun depicted in symbolic form in Bronze Age iconography is also a theme addressed in medieval Irish writings. This assuredly demonstrates the long survival of this particular belief.

The sacred nature of certain trees is also a widespread notion and is well documented in modern folklore. This too may be traced back at least as far as the Bronze Age as the exceptional Holme discovery demonstrates. The fact that this tree was deliberately inverted adds an additional cosmic significance to its deposition. Once again this was more than just an arboreal offering to some supernatural entity, it was also an expression of a sophisticated philosophy about the renewal of the cosmos and the relationship of heaven and earth and humanity's place therein. A similar idea is at the heart of those images of the sacred tree flanked by animals found on Iron Age belt hooks and on the Port sword where presumably it had some protective force as well.

It is surprising that such trees are all but absent in Bronze Age iconography but as the *axis mundi*, that link between worlds, it may have been expressed in other ways as the Goloring pillar would suggest. That Irish discovery at Shanaclogh, Co. Limerick, of a burnt tree root seemingly situated at the entrance to a small penannular ditched enclosure that contained some Bronze Age cremations illustrates how elusive the archaeological evidence may be. The concept of the sacred tree may well be even older than the Bronze Age.

The identification of sacred kings may present an even greater archaeological challenge. In fact it may never be possible to identify a sacral king with certainty for sacredness, as far as we know, leaves no archaeological trace. This is not to say that the institution did not exist – it most certainly did and its existence must have influenced other aspects of the social hierarchy in a significant manner. Warriors, poets and seers may have been an essential part of the entourage of such a person. Their sacral nature may have been expressed in very different ways in funerary contexts and clues may exist even in grave goods and aspects of burial practice that appear quite mundane to our eyes. It may be reflected in the presence of Otherworldly symbolism such as horses, birds or solar boats. Associated rituals may have included animal sacrifice and the ceremonial use of wagons or chariots.

No doubt some readers will be critical of an exercise that compares material from many different places and many different periods, but all of these themes were a part of the traditions of the Indo-European world. That they should have their origins in the Bronze Age, if not before, is therefore not surprising. It is to be expected that the archaeological evidence should be just as fragmented as the mythic themes that survive in medieval texts. In pursuing these themes we get a glimpse of traditions and beliefs that may once have had a wide currency in prehistoric Europe transcending the conceptual borders we impose on the past whether prompted by narrow nationalism or geographical determinism.

There are also those who question the fact that pagan beliefs and practices continued well into the medieval period in Ireland. That traces of them should survive well after the introduction of

Christianity to be included in the literary corpus is considered implausible. Yet there is a significant body of evidence to demonstrate that this was indeed the case.

To cite just a few examples: there is a famous but very brief reference to the sacred marriage in the *Annals of Connacht* in the year AD 1310. His foster-father takes Feidhlim Ó Conchobhair to an ancestral inauguration place of the O'Conors at Carnfree, near Rathcroghan, Co. Roscommon, to claim the kingship of Connacht. This medieval event was described as a *banais rígi* or king-ship marriage:

> Maelruanaid Mac Diarmata, seeing the exclusion of his foster-son from his patrimony ... determined, like the warrior he was, to take his foster-son boldly and make him king by force. So he carried him to Carnfree and installed him on the mound according to the practice of the saints, and of Da Conna of Assylin in particular; and he, Fedlimid mac Aeda meic Eogain, was proclaimed in a style as royal, as lordly and as public as any of his race from the time of Brian son of Eochu Muigmedoin till that day. And when Fedlimid mac Aeda meic Eogain had married the Province of Connacht his foster-father waited upon him during the night in the manner remembered by the old men and recorded in the old books; and this was the most splendid king-ship marriage ever celebrated in Connacht down to that day.[1]

Even though it is given a Christian gloss, this re-enactment of the archaic rite in the 14th century was conducted, it should be noted, *in the manner remembered by the old men and recorded in the old books*. This phrase and the use of the term king-ship marriage suggest the presence of a learned class well acquainted with ancient history and who treasured the memory of age-old ceremonial practices. It is not all surprising therefore that some two centuries earlier Giraldus Cambrensis was able to record details of an inauguration rite with its horse sacrifice in the territory of the Cenél Conaill in Donegal.

When in 1256, in response to a report that some 'sons of perdition' in Donegal were worshipping idols, Pope Alexander IV formally authorized Maol Pádraig Ó Scannail, bishop of Raphoe, to excommunicate them.² Sadly we have no certain idea what form these idols took but, between the activities of those perditious Donegal folk who continued pagan practices and the learned classes in Connacht who had no difficulty in recording features of a pre-Christian past, it is no surprise to find genuinely ancient mythic themes permeating the literature of the medieval world.³

Notes

Introduction

1. Waddell 1983; Waddell *et al.* 2009. Yeats' evocative image of the Otherworld is from his poem 'The Land of Heart's Desire'.
2. Newman 1997; Bhreathnach 1995.
3. Newman 2007.
4. Irregularity of form in medieval Irish myth has been studied by Borsje 2012.
5. Translation in Koch and Carey 1995, 167.
6. This argument was advanced in Waddell 2014, 118.
7. Littleton 1982.
8. Newman 2009.
9. Carey 2005.
10. Bradley 2005, 33.
11. Hutton 2009, 31.

Chapter 1

1. Byrne and Dillon 1937, 3.
2. Henderson 1899, 69.
3. Waddell *et al.* 2009.
4. Waddell 1988.
5. Ferguson 1882.
6. Byrne 1973, 77.
7. Newman 1997; Petrie 1839, 140, 184.
8. Gwynn 1903, 71, noted the parallels.
9. Ó Cathasaigh 2011.
10. Cross and Slover 1935, 153.
11. Bhreathnach 1998.
12. Lynn 1997; 2003. For a useful summary see Neill 2009, 182-97.
13. Mallory *et al.* 1999.
14. Mallory and Lynn 2002.
15. Mallory 2016; 1982; 1992.

16 De Grazia 2010.
17 Waddell 2005, 9ff.
18 Aitchison 1994, 302.
19 Declan Kiberd in a foreword to Boyd 2014, x.
20 From William Cowper's poem *Retirement* (1782): 'learn'd philologists, who chase a panting syllable through time and space, start it at home, and hunt it in the dark, to Gaul, to Greece, and into Noah's ark'.
21 Johnston 2013, 157.
22 Ó Cathasaigh 1984
23 Jackson 1961, 129.
24 Jordan 2001.
25 Fagan 2006.
26 Luce 1969.
27 Collina-Girard 2009.

Chapter 2

1 Meyer 1911, 101.
2 Ó Néill 1999.
3 O'Rahilly 1967, 272.
4 Lincoln 1981, 87; Mac Cana 1988, 339.
5 Edel 2015, 303, explores the variations in this story of the battle of the bulls in the three surviving recensions of the *Táin*.
6 Ó Máille 1928.
7 Mac Cana 1970, 85.
8 Herbert 1992, 264.
9 The etymology of the name has been questioned by Irslinger 2017 in a detailed study of Medb's many attributes.
10 Dumézil 1973, 81.
11 Gray 1982.
12 Ó Cathasaigh 1983.
13 Burke 1997, 59.
14 Barber and Barber 2004.
15 Tylor 1871.
16 Dundes 1988, 89.

Chapter 3

1 Recent studies include Jaski 2000; Doherty 2005 and Schot *et al.* 2011.
2 Mac Giolla Easpaig 2005.
3 O Daly 1975, 59 with emendation.

4 Dillon 1947; 1947a.
5 Watkins 1979.
6 Binchy 1970, 10.
7 Koch and Carey 1995, 158.
8 Dillon 1953, 56.
9 Mac Cana 1973a, 92, citing Pliny, *Historia Naturalis,* XVI. It has also been suggested, as he notes, that the *Serglige Con Culainn* account is borrowed from the description of Conaire's rite.
10 O'Connor 2013.
11 Koch and Carey 1995, 159.
12 Ó Cathasaigh 1996.
13 Translation in Herbert 2002, 260.
14 Herbert 1992, 270.
15 Translation in Herbert 2002, 261.
16 Bergin and Best 1938, 186-7.
17 Waddell 2014, 114.
18 De Pontfarcy 2002.
19 Mac Cana 2011, 161; Translation from Koch and Carey 1995, 387.
20 O'Meara 1951. There is some evidence that this ritual may have taken place at Doon Rock (Carraig an Dúnáin) near Donegal town: Ó Canann 2003.
21 Another inverted echo of this rite may occur in the mythic seduction of Europa by Zeus in the form of a bull: Sterckx 2013.
22 Puhvel 1970; Zaroff 2005.
23 Egeler 2012.
24 Gwynn 1912. See also comments by Carey 2005.
25 Bourgès 2006.
26 Fyfe and Levene 1997, 93; Tacitus *Histories* 2, 61.
27 Muller 1975.
28 Evans-Pritchard in his classic *The Divine Kingship of the Shilluk of the Nilotic Sudan* is credited with the statement 'the king of the Shilluk reigns but does not govern', often paraphrased, but as he indicated in a letter (*Man*, Vol. 6, 1971, 117-118) he borrowed it from Auguste Comte who quoted the maxim 'Le roi règne et ne gouverne pas'.
29 As pointed out by Binchy 1970, 9, who does note that most of the mythical 'kings of Ireland' were slain by their successors though motifs of revenge are invariably alleged for the deed. See Dalton 1970; 1972.
30 Schjødt 2010; Sundqvist 2012; Nygaard 2016.
31 Ström 1959.

32 Compare for example Chaney 1970 and Wormald 1986.
33 Beard *et al.* 1998, 55; Koptev 2012.
34 Palaima 1995.

Chapter 4

1   The line 'Where are now the warring kings?' comes from Yeats' poem 'The Song of the Happy Shepherd'.
2   Wrigley 1996, 126.
3   Gerloff 2010, 57.
4   Eogan 2001.
5   Jorge and Jorge 1993; Rodríguez-Corral 2015.
6   Graells 2012.
7   Warner 2006.
8   Cahill 2004.
9   Ireland 1992.
10 Jope 2000, 88, 252.
11 Uckelmann 2013, 40.
12 Ó Ríordáin 1997.
13 Newman 2007, 430.
14 Parker Pearson 1999, 56.
15 Carter *et al.* 2010.
16 Nagy 1992, 88.
17 Garrow and Gosden 2012, 226.
18 Parfitt 1995; Parfitt and Green 1987.
19 Stead in Parfitt 1995, 88.
20 There is a large body of literature on the Hochdorf grave including Biel 1982 and in English: Olivier 1999; Eggert 2007; Krausse 2007.
21 Watkins 1981.
22 Mac Cana 1973.
23 Green 2004, 163.
24 Krausse 1999.
25 Verger 2013.
26 Rees and Rees 1961, 193.
27 Howlett 2006, 73. This episode is the legend of the lighting of the Easter fire by Patrick on the Hill of Slane.
28 Singor 1991, in *Iliad* XIII: 689-700 and 790-802.
29 Treherne 1995.
30 Ní Dhonnchadha 2002, 296.
31 Mac Cana 2011, 327.

32 Newman 2007.
33 Hermann 2002.
34 Armit and Grant 2008.
35 Illustrated in Waddell 2014, 104.
36 This strange formulaic sequence of body parts, essentially flesh-bone-marrow, is also to be found with minor variations in charms and magical incantations in Old High German, Old Saxon, Vedic Sanskrit and Hittite and has prompted suggestions of an Indo-European source for this detail: Watkins 1995, 530. On Finn mac Cumaill: O'Rahilly 1946, 327ff; Nagy 1985, 21ff; Meyer 1904; Ó hÓgáin 1987.
37 Drumhallagh: Henry 1965, 124.
38 Ellis 1942.
39 Corbeill 2004, 7; Fischer 1965.
40 Quesada-Sanz 1998, 89, citing Almagro-Gorbea who has long been alert to the possible existence of sacral kingship (Almagro-Gorbea 1988).
41 Sørensen 2004.
42 Coles and Harding 1979, 238; Briard 1984; Needham *et al.* 2006.
43 Needham 2000.
44 Woodward and Hunter 2015, 235. Described as a 'royal burial' by Ashbee 1960, 76.
45 Needham 2000a, 190, and in Woodward and Hunter 2015, 260.
46 Bourgeois and van der Vaart-Verschoof 2017.
47 Sharples 2005.
48 Scarre 2013.

Chapter 5

1 Waddell 2014a.
2 O Daly 1975, 48.
3 Borsje 2009, 182.
4 A theme examined in Waddell 2014, 66; 2014a. This sort of subterranean testing of a warrior is reminiscent of the trials of the knight Owein in a cave at Saint Patrick's Purgatory on an island in Lough Derg, Co. Donegal. The accounts of the hellish horrors he faced and eventually survived were immensely popular in the medieval world. Its medieval usage is first recorded in the 12th century. Whether it had pre-Christian roots is uncertain but it may be a Christianized version of the kind of rituals suggested at Oweynagat: Rees and Rees 1961, 304; De Pontfarcy 1988.
5 Translation after Koch and Carey 1995, 117.
6 Watson 1986.

7   Carey 1988. Sayers 2012 provides a recent overview of the complexities of the early Irish Otherworld.
8   Davidson and Fisher 1996, Vol. 1, 30; Vol. 2, 35. Also Egeler 2013, 103.
9   Le Quellec and Sergent 2017, 114.
10 Carey 1983.
11 Koch and Carey 1995, 145.
12 Jackson 1942.
13 Bradley 1990.
14 Harrison 2004.
15 Trachsel 2005. The burial from Cazevieille is conveniently illustrated in a sketch in Cowen 1967, 419.
16 Stead 1995.
17 Dent 1985.
18 Lynn 1993.
19 Shepherd and Shepherd 2001.
20 Bradley *et al.* 2016.
21 Cahill and Sikora 2011, 244.
22 Longworth 1984, 47, 141.
23 Ó Ríordáin and Waddell 1993, 19, 33.
24 Nordberg 2009. The Tängelgårda stone is illustrated in Jones 1984, pl. 13.
25 Stokes 1893.
26 Carey 1994.
27 Lernez-de Wilde 1982, 104.
28 Ó Floinn 2009.
29 Megaw and Megaw 2001, 236.
30 Piggott and Daniel 1951, 20.
31 Duval 1977, 230; Jope 2000, 272.
32 Joy 2008; 2010, 32.
33 Koch 1992.
34 Kaul 2005.
35 Kristiansen 2010. He also notes two early Bronze Age shaft-hole axes from Hajdu Samson, Hungary, bearing stylized images of upright and inverted boats, that seem to indicate that this belief may have been current at a much earlier date. This would support the suggestion that inverted early Bronze Age urns in these islands were also allusions to the Otherworld.
36 Wirth 2006.
37 Kleinklein: Prüssing 1991, 50, no. 104; Fangel Torp: Kaul 1998, no. 128.
38 Wirth 2006, 342, fig. 10; Uckelmann 2013, 78, no. 89.

Chapter 6

1. FitzPatrick 2004, 57, 122, 148.
2. Schot 2011.
3. Bondarenko 2014a; Watson 1981.
4. Lucas 1963.
5. Bondarenko 2014, 44.
6. Ó Broin 1974; Muhr 2002.
7. O Daly 1960.
8. Muhr 2013.
9. Binchy 1971.
10. Ó Súilleabháin 1942, 281.
11. Wyss 1954; 1956.
12. Brennand *et al.* 2003.
13. Pryor 2001, 276.
14. Manning 1988.
15. Eliade 1958, 273; Coomaraswamy 1977.
16. Andrén 2014, 49.
17. Skoglund 2012.
18. Boughey and Vickerman 2003, 21, no. 598.
19. Tonnochy and Hawkes 1931.
20. Kaul 1998, 188.
21. Mac Cana 2011, 166.
22. Lorrio and Sánchez de Prado 2009, 483.
23. Marco Simón 1998, 107.
24. Garcia Quintela and Delpech 2013.
25. Green 2000; 2004; Lajoye 2016.
26. Braund 1999, 52; III 399-417 and I 444-446.
27. Sergent 1992.
28. Livens 1972; Pearce 2013.
29. James 1966.
30. Mallory and Adams 1997, 248; Hooke 2010; Cusack 2011, 19.
31. Bushnell 2008.
32. Eliade 1959, 36, 147.
33. Eson 2010.
34. Waddell 2014, 106.
35. Doherty 2005, 15.
36. Williams *et al.* 1996, 65, 154.
37. Kimmig 1965.
38. Post BX: Hope-Taylor 1977, 73, 258.

39 Andrén 2014, 43, 54, who also notes the interpretative difficulties.
40 Lynn 1997, 221.
41 Chapple 2010, 43, 91, pit C1935 dated to 1730-1536 BC.
42 Megaw 1970, 131.
43 Enright 2007.
44 Bémont 1979.
45 Powell 1971, 202.
46 Maier 2001.
47 Dillon 1973.
48 Stöllner 2014.
49 Ginoux 2007.
50 Jacobsthal 1944, 198.

Chapter 7

1 Mac Cana 1970, 85.
2 Gwynn 1924, 309.
3 Mac Cana 1988, 335.
4 As translated by Toner 1988.
5 Mac Cana 2011, 127. Translation in Hull 1968 and Ní Dhonnchadha 2002a, 173.
6 It has been argued that the image of Macha as a horse-like fertility goddess could be a medieval invention: Toner 2010. Her standing is considered in Waddell 2017.
7 Mac Mathúna 2014, 69.
8 Sterckx 1986, 40; 2009, 223; Green 1995, 47; Ford 2008, 35; Tolstoy 2016, 162. Not everyone accepts Rhiannon's divinity: Hemming 1998, for example, prefers to see explanations in folklore and history for the magical elements of her story.
9 McKenna 1980.
10 Mallory and Adams 2006, 432.
11 Hubert 1925.
12 Gricourt 1954; Dumézil 1954.
13 Green 1989, 17.
14 For example Euskirchen 1993; Hofeneder 2005.
15 Koch 2009, 30, 85; Koch 2010, 215, 262.
16 Tatár 2007.
17 Ólafsson 1995.
18 Harrison 2004, 144; Kristiansen and Larsson 2005.
19 Green 2006, 30.

20 Allen 1973.
21 Puhvel 1970, 167.
22 Edel 2015, 294-5; Gwynn 1924, 367.
23 Richmond 1954, 43.
24 Bendrey *et al.* 2013.
25 Ó Floinn 2001.
26 Coffey 1905.
27 Cahill Wilson *et al.* 2014, 141; Mapping Death Database: http://www.mappingdeathdb.ie/idlocs (retrieved 2-11-17).
28 Stead 1965, 89.
29 Mildenhall: Clarke 1939, 43, where an extended skeleton was flanked by the animals and accompanied by an iron sword, an axe and a gold torc. At Fordington the bones of a man and a horse along with a bronze bit were found in the 19th century: Cunliffe 1991, 505.
30 Lepaumier *et al.* 2009.
31 Hubert 1902.
32 http://www.inrap.fr/la-sepulture-aristocratique-de-warcq-une-exceptionnelle-tombe-char-gauloise-5357
33 Waddell 2014, 124.
34 Pollard 2017.
35 Needham 1991, 110, 334, 380. A calibrated radiocarbon date for the horse bones is cited by Bendrey *et al.* 2013: 1129–806 BC (OxA-3428).
36 Stead 1991, 27, 144.
37 Graham 2006, 167.
38 Cunliffe 1984, 538.
39 Grant 1991, 110.
40 McKinley *et al.* 2014, 61, 176.
41 Bayle and Salin 2013, 206.
42 Collins 1952.
43 Bendrey *et al.* 2010.
44 Ellis and Powell 2008, 22, 91.
45 Kaeser 2017.
46 Russell et al. 2014.
47 Méniel 2005.
48 Méniel 1992.
49 Jouin and Méniel 2000.
50 Sarry *et al.* 2016; Foucras 2014.
51 Poux 2003.
52 Giraud 2015.
53 Green 1992; 2004; Kruta 2012.

54 Metzner-Nebelsick and Nebelsick 1999.
55 Creighton 2000; 2005.
56 Green 2004, 163.
57 As Creighton 2000, 129, indicates.

Epilogue

1 Freeman 1944, 223.
2 Sheehy 1965, 251.
3 Other examples of pagan activity in medieval times are cited in Waddell 2011 and 2017.

References

Aitchison, N. B. 1994. *Armagh and the Royal Centres in Early Medieval Ireland: monuments, cosmology and the past*. Woodbridge: Boydell and Brewer.

Allen, D. F. 1973. Temples or shrines on Gaulish coins. *Antiquaries Journal* 53, 71–4.

Almagro-Gorbea, M. 1988. Société et commerce méditerranéen dans la péninsule Ibérique aux VII–Ve siècles. In *Les Princes Celtes et la Méditerranée*, 71–9. Paris: La Documentation Française.

Andrén, A. 2014. *Tracing Old Norse Cosmology. The World Tree, Middle Earth, and the Sun from Archaeological Perspectives*. Lund: Nordic Academic Press.

Aner, E. and Kersten, K. 1976. *Die Funde der älteren Bronzezeit des nordischen Kreises in Dänemark, Schleswig-Holstein und Niedersachsen 2*. Copenhagen: National Museum of Denmark.

Armit, I. and Grant, P. 2008. Gesture politics and the art of ambiguity: the Iron Age statue from Hirschlanden. *Antiquity* 82, 409–22.

Armstrong, E. C. R. 1933. *Catalogue of Irish Gold Ornaments in the Collection of the Royal Irish Academy*. Dublin: Stationery Office.

Ashbee, P. 1960. *The Bronze Age Round Barrow in Britain*. London: Phoenix House.

Auboyer, J. 1959. Le caractère royal et divin du trône dans l'Inde ancienne. In *La regalità sacra. The sacral kingship. Contributions to the central theme of the VIIIth International Congress for the History of Religions (Rome, April 1955)*, 181–88. Leiden: E. J. Brill.

Barber, E. J. W and Barber, P. 2004. *When They Severed Earth From Sky: how the Human Mind Shapes Myth*. Princeton: Princeton University Press.

Bayle, G. and Salin, M. 2013. Les dépôts particuliers d'équidés à l'âge de Fer en région Centre. In G. Auxiette and P. Méniel (eds), *Les dépôts d'ossements animaux en France, de la fouille à l'interprétation*, 201–8. Autun: Éditions Mergoil.

Beard, M., North, J. and Price, S. 1998. *Religions of Rome: Volume 1, a history*. Cambridge: Cambridge University Press.

Bémont, C. 1979. Le bassin de Gundestrup: remarques sur les décors végétaux. *Études Celtiques* 16, 69–99.
Bendrey, R., Leach, S. and Clark, K. 2010. New light on an old rite: reanalysis of an Iron Age burial group from Blewburton Hill, Oxfordshire. In J. Morris and M. Maltby (eds), *Integrating Social and Environmental Archaeologies: reconsidering deposition*, 33–44. Oxford: British Archaeological Report S2077.
Bendrey, R., Thorpe, N., Outram, A. and van Wijngaarden-Bakker, L. H. 2013. The Origins of Domestic Horses in Northwest Europe: new Direct Dates on the Horses of Newgrange, Ireland. *Proceedings of the Prehistoric Society* 79, 1–13.
Bergin, O. and Best, R. I. 1938. Tochmarc Étaíne. *Ériu* 12, 137–96.
Bhreathnach, E. 1995. *Tara: a select bibliography.* Dublin: Royal Irish Academy.
Bhreathnach, E. 1998. The *tech midchúarta*, 'the house of the mead-circuit': feasting, royal circuits and the king's court in early Ireland. *Archaeology Ireland* 12 (4), 20–2.
Biel, J. 1982. Ein Fürstengrabhügel der späten Hallstattzeit bei Eberdingen-Hochdorf, Kr. Ludwigsburg, Baden-Württemberg. *Germania* 60, 61–104.
Binchy, D. A. 1970. *Celtic and Anglo-Saxon Kingship. The O'Donnell Lectures for 1967–8.* Oxford: Oxford University Press.
Binchy, D. A. 1971. An archaic legal poem. *Celtica* 152–68.
Bondarenko, G. 2014. The significance of pentads in Early Irish and Indian Sources: the case of five directions. In G. Bondarenko (ed.), *Studies in Irish Mythology,* 43–56. Berlin: curach bhán publications.
Bondarenko, G. 2014a. The five primeval trees in Early Irish, Gnostic, and Manichaean cosmologies. In G. Bondarenko (ed.), *Studies in Irish Mythology,* 57–68. Berlin: curach bhán publications.
Borsje, J. 2009. Supernatural Threats to Kings: Exploration of a Motif in the Ulster Cycle and in Other Medieval Irish Tales. In R. Ó hUiginn and B. Ó Catháin (eds), *Ulidia 2. Proceedings of the Second International Conference on the Ulster Cycle of Tales,* 173–94. Maynooth: An Sagart.
Borsje, J. 2012. *The Celtic Evil Eye and Related Mythological Motifs in Medieval Ireland.* Louvain: Peeters.
Boughey, K. J. S. and Vickerman, E. A. 2003. *Prehistoric Rock Art of the West Riding: cup-and-ring-marked rocks of the valleys of the Aire, Wharfe, Washburn and Nidd.* Leeds: West Yorkshire Archaeological Service.
Bourgeois, Q. and van der Vaart-Verschoof, S. 2017. A practice perspective. Understanding Early Iron Age elite burials in the southern Netherlands through event-based analysis. In R. Schumann and S. van der Vaart-Verschoof (eds), *Connecting Elites and Regions. Perspectives on Contacts,*

Relations and Differentiation during the Early Iron Age Hallstatt C Period in Northwest and Central Europe, 305–18. Leiden: Sidestone.

Bourgès, A. Y. 2006. Melor. In J. T. Koch (ed.), *Celtic Culture. A Historical Encyclopedia* 4, 1288–9. Santa Barbara: ABC-CLIO.

Boyd. M. (ed.) 2014. *Coire Sois, The Cauldron of Knowledge: a companion to early Irish Saga, Tomás Ó Cathasaigh*. Notre Dame: University of Notre Dame Press.

Bradley, R. 1990. *The Passage of Arms: an archaeological analysis of prehistoric hoards and votive deposits*. Cambridge: Cambridge University Press.

Bradley, R., Rogers, A., Fraser, S. and Watson, A. 2016. Maritime havens in earlier prehistoric Britain. *Proceedings of the Prehistoric Society* 82, 125–59.

Braund, S. H. 1999. *Lucan Civil War*. Oxford: Oxford University Press.

Brennand, M. and Taylor, M. 2003. The survey and excavation of a Bronze Age timber circle at Holme-next-the-Sea, Norfolk, 1998–9. *Proceedings of the Prehistoric Society* 69, 1–84.

Briard, J. 1984. *Les tumulus d'Armorique*. Paris: Picard.

Burke, P. 1997. *Varieties of Cultural History*. Cambridge: Polity Press.

Bushnell, L. 2008. The wild goat-and-tree icon and its special significance for ancient Cyprus. In G. Papantoniou (ed.), *POCA 2005. Postgraduate Cypriot Archaeology. Proceedings of the Fifth Annual Meeting of Young Researchers on Cypriot Archaeology, Department of Classics, Trinity College, Dublin, 21–22 October 2005*, 65–76. Oxford: British Archaeological Report S1803.

Byrne, F. J. 1973. *Irish Kings and High-Kings*. London: Batsford.

Byrne, M. E. and Dillon, M. 1937. Táin Bó Fraich. *Études Celtiques* 2, 1–27.

Cahill, M. 2004. The gold beads from Tumna, Co. Roscommon. In H. Roche, E. Grogan, J. Bradley, J. Coles and B. Raftery (eds), *From Megaliths to Metal. Essays in Honour of George Eogan*, 99–108. Oxford: Oxbow Books.

Cahill, M. and Sikora, M. (eds), 2011. *Breaking Ground, Finding Graves – Reports on the Excavations of Burials by the National Museum of Ireland, 1927–2006. Volume 1*. Dublin: National Museum of Ireland.

Cahill Wilson, J., Standish, C. and O'Brien, E. 2014. Investigating mobility and migration in the later Irish Iron Age. *Discovery Programme Reports* 8, 127–49.

Carey, J. 1983. The location of the Otherworld in Irish tradition. *Éigse* 19, 36–43. Reprinted in J. Wooding (ed.), 2000. *The Otherworld Voyage in Early Irish Literature. An Anthology of Criticism*. Dublin: Four Courts Press.

Carey, J. 1988. Sequence and Causation in *Echtra Nerai*. *Ériu* 39, 67–74.

Carey, J. 1994. The sun's night journey: a Pharaonic image in medieval Ireland. *Journal of the Warburg and Courtauld Institutes* 57, 14–34.

Carey, J. 2005. Tara and the supernatural. In E. Bhreathnach (ed.), *The Kingship and Landscape of Tara*, 32–48. Dublin: Four Courts Press.

Carter, S., Hunter, F. and Smith, A. 2010. A 5th century BC Iron Age chariot burial from Newbridge, Edinburgh. *Proceedings of the Prehistoric Society* 76, 31–74.

Chaney, W. A. 1970. *The Cult of Kingship in Anglo-Saxon England*. Manchester: Manchester University Press.

Chapple, R. M. 2010. *The Excavation of an Enclosed Middle Bronze Age Cemetery at Gransha, Co. Londonderry, Northern Ireland*. Oxford: British Archaeological Report 521.

Clarke, R. R. 1939. The Iron Age in Norfolk and Suffolk. *Archaeological Journal* 96, 1–113.

Coffey, G. 1905. On the excavation of a tumulus near Loughrea. *Proceedings of the Royal Irish Academy* 25C, 14–20.

Coles, J. and Harding, A. F. 1979. *The Bronze Age in Europe*. London: Methuen.

Collina-Girard, J. 2009. *L'Atlantide retrouvée? Enquête scientifique autour d'un mythe*. Paris: Éditions Belin.

Collins, A. E. P. 1952. Excavations on Blewburton Hill, 1948 and 1949. *Berkshire Archaeological Journal* 53, 21–64.

Coomaraswamy, A. K. 1977. The inverted tree. In R. Lipsey (ed.), *Coomaraswamy. 1: Selected Papers. Traditional Art and Symbolism*, 376–404. Princeton: Princeton University Press.

Corbeill, A. 2004. *Nature Embodied: gesture in ancient Rome*. Princeton: Princeton University Press.

Cowen, J. D. 1967. The Hallstatt sword of bronze: on the Continent and in Britain. *Proceedings of the Prehistoric Society* 33, 377–454.

Creighton, J. 2000. *Coins and Power in Late Iron Age Britain*. Cambridge: Cambridge University Press.

Creighton, J. 2005. Gold, ritual and kingship. In C. Haselgrove and D. Wigg-Wolf (eds), *Iron Age Coinage and Ritual Practices*, 69–84. Mainz: Philipp von Zabern.

Cross, T. P. and Slover, C. H. 1935. *Ancient Irish Tales*. London: Harrap.

Cunliffe, B. 1984. *Danebury: an Iron Age hillfort in Hampshire, Volume 2, The excavations, 1969–1978: the finds*. London: Council for British Archaeology Research Report 52.

Cunliffe, B. 1991. *Iron Age Communities in Britain* (3rd edn). London: Routledge.

Cusack, C. M. 2011. *The Sacred Tree: ancient and medieval manifestations*. Newcastle upon Tyne: Cambridge Scholars.

Dalton, G. F. 1970. The ritual killing of the Irish Kings. *Folklore* 81, 1–22.

Dalton, G. F. 1972. Kings dying on Tuesday. *Folklore* 83, 220–4.
Davidson, H. E. and Fisher, P. 1996. *Saxo Grammaticus. The History of the Danes Books I–IX.* Woodbridge: Boydell and Brewer.
De Grazia, M. 2010. Anachronism. In B. Cummings and J. Simpson (eds), *Cultural Reformations: medieval and Renaissance in literary history,* 13–32. Oxford: Oxford University Press.
Dent, J. 1985. Three cart burials from Wetwang, Yorkshire. *Antiquity* 59, 85–92.
De Pontfarcy, Y. 1988. The historical background to the pilgrimage to Lough Derg. In M. Haren and Y. de Pontfarcy (eds), *The Medieval Pilgrimage to St Patrick's Purgatory: Lough Derg and the European tradition,* 7–34. Enniskillen: Clogher Historical Society.
De Pontfarcy, Y. 2002. The sovereignty of Paeonia. In M. Richter and J-M. Picard (eds), *Ogma. Essays in Celtic studies in honour of Próinséas Ní Chatháin,* 145–50. Dublin: Four Courts Press.
Dillon, M. 1947. The Hindu Act of Truth in Celtic tradition. *Modern Philology* 44, 137–40.
Dillon, M. 1947a. The archaism of Irish tradition. *Proceedings of the British Academy* 33, 245–64.
Dillon, M. 1953. The wasting sickness of Cu Chulainn. *Scottish Gaelic Studies* 7, 47–88.
Dillon, M. 1973. The consecration of Irish kings. *Celtica* 10, 1–8.
Doherty, C. 2005. Kingship in Early Ireland. In E. Bhreathnach (ed.), *The Kingship and Landscape of Tara,* 3–31. Dublin: Four Courts Press.
Dumézil, G. 1954. Le trio des Macha. *Revue de l'histoire des religions* 146, 5–17.
Dumézil, G. 1973. *The Destiny of a King.* Trans. A. Hiltebeitel. Chicago: University of Chicago Press.
Dundes, A. 1988. *The Flood Myth.* Berkeley: University of California Press.
Duval, P-M. 1975. A propos de la signification des images monétaires gauloises. *Comptes rendus des séances de l'Académie des Inscriptions et Belles-Lettres* 119, 241–55.
Duval, P-M. 1977. *Les Celtes.* Paris: Gallimard.
Duval, P-M. 1987. *Monnaies Gauloises et mythes celtiques.* Paris: Hermann.
Edel, D. 2015. *Inside the Táin. Exploring Cú Chulainn, Fergus, Ailill, and Medb.* Berlin: curach bhán publications.
Egeler, M. 2012. Some thoughts on 'Goddess Medb' and her typological context. *Zeitschrift für celtische Philologie* 59, 67–96.

Egeler, M. 2013. *Celtic Influences in Germanic Religion. A Survey.* Munich: Herbert Utz.

Eggert, M. K. H. 2007. The Hochdorf dead. Comments on the mode of archaeological interpretation. In R. Karl and D. Stifter (eds), *The Celtic World: critical concepts in historical studies, Vol. 2, Celtic archaeology,* 180–96. London: Routledge.

Eliade, M. 1958. *Patterns in Comparative Religion.* New York: Sheed and Ward.

Eliade, M. 1959. *The Sacred and the Profane. The Nature of Religion.* San Diego: Harcourt.

Ellis, C. and Powell, A. B. 2008. *An Iron Age Settlement Outside Battlesbury Hillfort, Warminster, and Sites along the Southern Range Road.* Salisbury: Wessex Archaeology Report 22.

Ellis, H. R. 1942. Sigurd in the Art of the Viking Age. *Antiquity* 16, 216–36.

Enright, M. J. 2007. Ritual and technology in the Iron Age: an initiation scene on the Gundestrup cauldron. In S. O. Glosecki (ed.), *Myth in Early Northwest Europe,* 105–20. Tempe: Arizona Center for Medieval and Renaissance Studies.

Eogan, G. 2001. A composite late Bronze Age object from Roscommon, Ireland. In W. H. Metz, B. L. van Beek and H. Steegstra (eds), *Patina. Essays presented to Jay Jordan Butler on the occasion of his 80th birthday,* 231–40. Groningen: Metz, Van Beek and Steegstra.

Eson, L. 2010. Odin and Merlin: threefold death and the world tree. *Western Folklore* 69, 85–107.

Euskirchen, M. 1993. Epona. *Bericht der Römisch-Germanischen Kommission* 74, 607–838.

Fagan, G. G. 2006. Diagnosing pseudoarchaeology. In G. G. Fagan (ed.), *Archaeological Fantasies: how pseudoarchaeology misrepresents the past and misleads the public.* London: Routledge.

Ferguson, S. 1882. On the legend of Dathi. *Proceedings of the Royal Irish Academy* 16, 167–84.

Fischer, H. 1965. The use of gesture in preparing medicaments and healing. *History of Religions* 5, 18–53.

FitzPatrick, E. 2004. *Royal Inauguration in Gaelic Ireland c. 1100–1600. A Cultural Landscape Study.* Woodbridge: Boydell Press.

Ford, P. K. 2008. *The Mabinogi and Other Medieval Welsh Tales.* Berkeley: University of California Press.

Foucras, S. 2014. Les équidés arvernes et le phénomène des fosses à chevaux (Puy-de-Dôme, France). In A. Gardeisen & C. Chandezon (eds), *Équidés et bovidés de la Méditerranée antique. Rites et combats. Jeux et savoirs*, 141–55. Lattes: CNRS.

Freeman, A. M. 1944. *Annála Connacht. The Annals of Connacht (A. D. 1224–1544)*. Dublin: Dublin Institute for Advanced Studies.

Fritsch, T. 2010. Ahnen – Helden – Götter. Die grossplastischen Skulpturen der frühen Kelten. In Terrex gGmbH (ed.), *Kelten und Römer im Sankt Wendeler Land. Die Ausgrabungen der TERREX gGmbH am 'Hunnenring' und im vicus Wareswald*, 13650. Marpingen: Edition Schaumberg.

Fyfe, W. H. and Levene, D. S. (eds), 1997. *Tacitus. The Histories*. Oxford: Oxford University Press.

García Quintela, M. V. and Delpech, F. 2013. *El árbol de Guernica. Memoria indoeuropea de los ritos vascos de soberanía*. Madrid: Abada Editores.

Garrow, D. and Gosden, C. 2012. *Technologies of Enchantment? Exploring Celtic Art: 400 BC to AD 100*. Oxford: Oxford University Press.

Gerloff, S. 2010. *Atlantic Cauldrons and Buckets of the Late Bronze Age and Early Iron Ages in Western Europe*. Praehistorische Bronzefunde II:18. Stuttgart: Franz Steiner Verlag.

Ginoux, N. 2007. *Le thème symbolique de 'la paire de dragons' sur les fourreaux celtiques (IVe–IIe siècles avant J.-C.)*. Oxford: British Archaeological Report S1702.

Giraud, P. 2015. *L'habitat et la nécropole celtes de Cagny: 'carrefour Philippe'*. Caen: Département du Calvados Service Archéologie.

Graells, R. 2012. Discos-coraza de la Península Ibérica (s. VI–IV a. C.). *Jahrbuch des Römisch-Germanischen Zentralmuseums* 59, 85–244.

Graham, A. H. 2006. *Excavations at Barton Field, Tarrant Hinton, Dorset, 1968–1984: excavation by R.G. Tanner and A.G. Giles, Wimborne Archaeological Group*. Dorchester: Dorset Natural History and Archaeological Society.

Grant, A. 1991. Economic or symbolic? Animals and ritual behaviour. In. P. Garwood, D. Jennings, R. Skeates and J. Toms (eds), *Sacred and Profane: proceedings of a conference on archaeology, ritual and religion, Oxford, 1989*, 109–14. Oxford: Oxford University Committee for Archaeology.

Gray, E. A. 1982. *Cath Maige Tuired. The second battle of Mag Tuired*. London: Irish Texts Society.

Green, M. 1989. *Symbol and Image in Celtic Religious Art*. London: Routledge.

Green, M. 1992. *Animals in Celtic Life and Myth*. London: Routledge.

Green, M. 1995. *Celtic Goddesses: warriors, virgins, and mothers*. London: British Museum Press.

Green, M. A. 2000. *Seeing the Wood for the Trees: the symbolism of trees and wood in ancient Gaul and Britain*. Aberystwyth: University of Wales Centre for Advanced Welsh and Celtic Studies.

Green, M. A. 2004. *An Archaeology of Images. Iconology and Cosmology in Iron Age and Roman Europe*. London: Routledge.

Green, M. A. 2006. Metaphors, meaning and money: contextualising some symbols on Iron Age coins. In P. de Jersey (ed.), *Celtic Coinage: new discoveries and new discussion*, 29–40. Oxford: British Archaeological Repor S1532.

Gricourt, J. 1954. Epona – Rhiannon – Macha. *Ogam* 6, 25–40.

Gwynn, E. 1903. *The Metrical Dindshenchas Part I*. Dublin: School of Celtic Studies – Dublin Institute for Advanced Studies 1991 reprint.

Gwynn, E. 1924. *The Metrical Dindshenchas Part IV*. Dublin: School of Celtic Studies – Dublin Institute for Advanced Studies 1991 reprint.

Gwynn, L. 1912. De Síl Chonairi Móir. *Ériu* 6, 130–43.

Hansen, L. 2010. *Hochdorf VIII. Die Goldfunde und Trachtbeigaben des späthallstattzeitlichen Fürstengrabes von Eberdingen-Hochdorf (Kr. Ludwigsburg)*. Stuttgart: Konrad Theiss.

Harrison, R. J. 2004. *Symbols and Warriors. Images of the European Bronze Age*. Bristol: Western Academic and Specialist Press.

Hemming, J. 1998. Reflections on Rhiannon and the Horse Episodes in 'Pwyll'. *Western Folklore* 57 (1), 19–40.

Henderson, G. 1899. *Fled Bricrend: The Feast of Bricriu*. London: Irish Texts Society.

Henry, F. 1965. *Irish Art in the Early Christian Period (to 800 A.D.)*. London: Methuen.

Herbert, M. 1992. Goddess and king: the sacred marriage in early Ireland. *Cosmos* 7, 264–75.

Herbert, M. 2002. Society and myth, c. 700–1300. In A. Bourke, M. Kilfeather, M. Luddy, M. Mac Curtain, G. Meaney, M. Ní Dhonnchadha, M. O'Dowd and C. Wills (eds), *The Field Day Anthology of Irish Writing, Vol. 4. Irish Women's Writings and Traditions*, 250–61. Cork: Cork University Press.

Hermann, F-R. 2002. Der Glauberg, Fürstensitz, Fürstengräber und Heiligtum. In H. Baitinger and B. Pinsker (eds), *Das Ratsel der Kelten von Glauberg: Glaube, Mythos, Wirklichkeit*, 90–111. Stuttgart: Theiss.

Hofeneder, A. 2005. Die Göttin Epona in der antiken Literatur. In W. Spickermann and R. Wiegels (eds), *Keltische Götter im Römischen Reich*, 29–46. Möhnesee: Bibliopolis.

Hooke, D. 2010. *Trees in Anglo-Saxon England. Literature, Lore and Landscape*. Woodbridge: Boydell Press.

Hope-Taylor, B. 1977. *Yeavering. An Anglo-British Centre of Early Northumbria*. London: English Heritage.

Howlett, D. 2006. *Muirchú Moccu Macthéni's 'Vita Sancti Patricii': Life of Saint Patrick*. Dublin: Four Courts Press.

Hubert, H. 1902. Sépulture à char de Nanterre. *Anthropologie* 13, 66–73.

Hubert, H. 1925. Le mythe d'Epona. In *Mélanges linguistiques offerts à M. J. Vendryes par ses amis et ses élèves*, 187–98. Paris: Champion.

Hull, V. 1968. *Noínden Ulad:* The Debility of the Ulidians. *Celtica* 8, 1–42.

Hutton, R. 2009. *Blood and Mistletoe. The History of the Druids in Britain*. New Haven: Yale University Press.

Ireland, A. 1992. The finding of the 'Clonmacnoise' gold torcs. *Proceedings of the Royal Irish Academy* 92C, 123–46.

Irslinger, B. 2017. Medb, 'the intoxicating one'? (Re-)constructing the past through etymology. In M. B. Ó Mainnín and G. Toner (eds), *Ulidia 4. Proceedings of the Fourth International Conference on the Ulster Cycle of Tales*, 38–94. Dublin: Four Courts Press.

Jackson, K. H. 1942. The adventure of Laeghaire Mac Crimhthainn. *Speculum* 17, 377–89.

Jackson, K. H. 1961. *The International Popular Tale and Early Welsh Tradition*. Cardiff: University of Wales Press

Jackson, K. H. 1964. *The Oldest Irish Tradition: a window on the Iron Age*. Cambridge: Cambridge University Press.

Jacobsthal, P. 1944. *Early Celtic Art*. Oxford: Clarendon Press.

James, E. O. 1966. *The Tree of Life. An Archaeological Study*. Leiden: E. J. Brill.

Jaski, B. 2000. *Early Irish Kingship and Succession*. Dublin: Four Courts Press.

Johnston, E. 2013. *Literacy and Identity in Early Medieval Ireland*. Woodbridge: Boydell Press.

Jones, G. 1984. *A History of the Vikings*. Oxford: Oxford University Press.

Jope, E. M. 2000. *Early Celtic Art in the British Isles*. Oxford: Oxford University Press.

Jordan, P. 2001. *The Atlantis Syndrome*. Stroud: Sutton.

Jorge, V. Oliveira and Jorge, S. Oliveira. 1993. Statues-menhirs et stèles du nord du Portugal. In J. Briard and A. Duval (eds), *Les représentations humaines du Néolithique à l'Âge du Fer*, 29–43. Paris: Éditions du Comité des Travaux Historiques et Scientifiques.

Jouin, M. and Méniel, P. 2000. Les dépôts animaux et le *fanum* gallo-romain de Vertault (Côte-d'Or). *Revue Archéologique de l'Est* 50, 119–216.

Joy, J. 2008. Reflections on Celtic Art: a re-examination of mirror decoration. In D. Garrow, C. Gosden and J. D. Hill (eds), *Rethinking Celtic Art*, 78–99. Oxford: Oxbow Books.

Joy, J. 2010. *Iron Age Mirrors. A Biographical Approach.* Oxford: British Archaeological Report 518.

Kaeser, M-A. 2017. La Tène. Nouvelles recherches, nouvelles interprétations. *Antiquité. Le Magazine de L'Antiquité européenne* 8, 48–59.

Kaul, F. 1998. *Ships on Bronzes. A Study in Bronze Age Religion and Iconography.* Copenhagen: National Museum of Denmark.

Kaul, F. 2005. Bronze Age tripartite cosmologies. *Praehistorische Zeitschrift* 80, 135–48.

Kimmig, W. 1965. Zur Interpretation der Opferszene auf dem Gundestrup-Kessel. *Fundberichte aus Schwaben* 17, 135–43.

Koch, J. T. 1992. Further to *Tongu do dia toinges mo thuath,* etc. *Études Celtiques* 29, 249–61.

Koch, J. T. 2009. *Tartessian. Celtic in the South-West at the Dawn of History.* Aberystwyth: Celtic Studies Publications.

Koch, J. T. 2010. Paradigm shift? Interpreting Tartessian as Celtic. In B. Cunliffe and J. T. Koch (eds), *Celtic from the West. Alternative Perspectives from Archeology, Genetics, Language and Literature*, 185–301. Oxford: Oxbow Books.

Koch, J. T and Carey, J. 1995. *The Celtic Heroic Age. Literary Sources for Ancient Celtic Europe and Early Ireland and Wales.* Malden: Celtic Studies Publications.

Koptev, A. 2012. *Rex Sacrorum*: The Roman king in space and time. *Ollodagos: Actes de la Société Belge d'Études Celtiques* 27, 51–130.

Krausse, D. 1999. Der 'Keltenfürst' von Hochdorf. *Archäologisches Korrespondenzblatt* 29, 339–58.

Krausse, D. 2007. The 'Celtic Prince' of Hochdorf: village-elder or sacred king? Pretence and reality of the so-called 'cultural anthropological' Hallstatt archaeology. In R. Karl and D. Stifter (eds), *The Celtic World: critical concepts in historical studies, Vol. 2, Celtic archaeology*, 197–229. London: Routledge.

Kristiansen, K. 2010. Rock art and religion. The sun journey in Indo-European mythology and Bronze Age rock art. In A. C. Fredell, K. Kristiansen and F. Criado Boado (eds), *Representations and Communications. Creating an Archaeological Matrix of Late Prehistoric Rock Art*, 93–115. Oxford: Oxbow Books.

Kristiansen, K. and Larsson, T. B. 2005. *The Rise of Bronze Age Society. Travels, Transmissions and Transformations.* Cambridge: Cambridge University Press.

Kruta, V. 2012. La place et la signification du cheval dans l'imagerie celtique. *Études Celtiques* 38, 43–59.

Lajoye, P. 2016. *L'arbre du monde. La cosmologie celte.* Paris: CNRS Éditions.

Lawson, A. J. 2007. *Chalkland. An archaeology of Stonehenge and its region.* Salisbury: Hobnob Press.

Lepaumier, H., Giazzon, D. and Chanson, K. 2009. Une tombe à char 'Les Pleines', Orval (Manche). *L'Archéologue* 102, 22–4.

Le Quellec, J-L. and Sergent, B. 2017. *Dictionnaire critique de mythologie.* Paris: CNRS Éditions.

Lernez-de Wilde, M. L. 1982. Le 'Style de Cheshire Cat', un phénomène caractéristique de l'art celtique. In P-M. Duval and V. Kruta (eds), *L'Art Celtique de la Période d'Expansion,* 101–23. Geneva: Droz.

Lincoln, B. 1981. *Priests, Warriors, and Cattle. A Study in the Ecology of Religions.* Berkeley: University of California Press.

Littleton, C. Scott. 1982 From swords in the earth to the sword in the stone: a possible reflection of an Alano-Sarmatian rite of passage in the Arthurian tradition. In E. C. Polomé (ed.), *Homage to Georges Dumézil,* 53–67. Washington: Journal of Indo-European Studies Monograph 3.

Livens, R. G. 1972. Who was Korisios? *Antiquity* 46, 56–8.

Longworth, I. H. 1984. *Collared Urns of the Bronze Age in Great Britain and Ireland.* Cambridge: Cambridge University Press.

Lorrio, A. J. and Sánchez de Prado, M.D. 2009. *La necrópolis celtibérica de Arcóbriga (Monreal de Ariza, Zaragoza).* Zaragoza: Institución 'Fernando el Católico'.

Lucas, A. T. 1963. The sacred trees of Ireland. *Journal of the Cork Historical and Archaeological Society* 68, 16–54.

Luce, J. V. 1969. *The end of Atlantis: new light on an old legend.* London: Thames and Hudson.

Lynn, C. J. 1993. House-urns in Ireland? *Ulster Journal of Archaeology* 56, 70–7.

Lynn, C. J. 1997. *Excavations at Navan Fort 1961–71 by D.M. Waterman.* Belfast: HMSO.

Lynn, C. J. 2002. Navan Fort site C excavations, May 2000, interim report no. 2. *Emania* 19, 5–18.

Lynn, C. J. 2003. *Navan Fort. Archaeology and Myth.* Bray: Wordwell.

Macalister, R. A. S. 1919. Temair Breg: a study of the remains and traditions of Tara. *Proceedings of the Royal Irish Academy* 34C, 231–399.

Mac Cana, P. 1970. *Celtic Mythology.* London: Hamlyn.

Mac Cana, P. 1973. The *topos* of the single sandal in Irish tradition. *Celtica* 10, 160–6.

Mac Cana, P. 1973a. Conservation and innovation in early Irish literature. *Études Celtiques* 13, 61–118.

Mac Cana, P. 1988. Placenames and mythology in Irish tradition: places, pilgrimages and things. In G. W. MacLennan (ed.), *Proceedings of the First North American Congress of Celtic Studies held at Ottawa from 26th–30th March, 1986*, 319–41. Ottawa: University of Ottawa.

Mac Cana, P. 2011. *The Cult of the Sacred Centre. Essays on Celtic Ideology*. Dublin: School of Celtic Studies – Dublin Institute for Advanced Studies.

Mac Giolla Easpaig, D. 2005. Significance and etymology of the placename *Temair*. In E. Bhreathnach (ed.), *The Kingship and Landscape of Tara*, 423–48. Dublin: Four Courts Press.

Mac Mathúna, S. 2014. The relationship of the chthonic world in early Ireland to chaos and cosmos. In J. Borsje, A. Dooley, S. Mac Mathúna and G. Toner (eds), *Celtic Cosmology. Perspectives from Ireland and Scotland*, 53–76. Toronto: Pontifical Institute of Medieval Studies.

Maier, F. 2001. Eiche und Efeu. Zu einer Rekonstruktion des Kultbäumchens aus Manching. *Germania* 79, 297–307.

Mallory, J. P. 1982. The sword of the Ulster Cycle. In B.G. Scott (ed.), *Studies on Early Ireland: essays in honour of M.V. Duignan*, 99–114. Belfast: AYIA.

Mallory, J. P. [1985]. *Navan Fort. The Ancient Capital of Ulster*. Belfast: Ulster Archaeological Society.

Mallory, J. P. 1992. The world of Cú Chulainn: the archaeology of *Táin Bó Cúailnge*. In J. P. Mallory (ed.), *Aspects of the Táin*, 103–59. Belfast: December Publications.

Mallory, J. P. 2016. *In Search of the Irish Dreamtime. Archaeology and Early Irish Literature*. London: Thames and Hudson.

Mallory, J. P. and Adams, D. Q. (eds), 1967. *Encyclopedia of Indo-European Culture*. London: Fitzroy Dearborn.

Mallory, J. P. and Adams, D. Q. 2006. *The Oxford Introduction to Proto-Indo-European and the Proto-Indo-European World*. Oxford: Oxford University Press.

Mallory, J. P., Brown, D. M. and Baillie, M. G. L. 1999. Dating Navan Fort. *Antiquity* 73, 427–31.

Mallory, J. P and Lynn, C. J. 2002. Recent excavations and speculations on the Navan complex. *Antiquity* 76, 532–41.

Manning, C. 1988. A Note on Sacred Trees. *Emania* 5, 34–5.

Mapping Death Database: http://www.mappingdeathdb.ie/idlocs (retrieved 22-5-16).

Marco-Simón, F. 1998. *Die Religion im keltischen Hispanien*. Budapest: Archaeolingua.

McKenna, C. A. 1980. The theme of sovereignty in *Pwyll*. *Bulletin of the Board of Celtic Studies* 29, 35–52.
McKinley, J. I., Leivers, M., Schuster, J., Marshall, P., Barclay, A. J. and Stoodley, N. 2014. *Cliffs End Farm, Isle of Thanet, Kent. A mortuary and ritual site of the Bronze Age, Iron Age and Anglo-Saxon period with evidence for long distance maritime mobility*. Salisbury: Wessex Archaeology Report 31.
Megaw, J. V. S 1970. *Art of the European Iron Age. A Study of the Elusive Image*. Bath: Adams and Dart.
Megaw, R. and Megaw, V. 2001. *Celtic Art. From its Beginnings to the Book of Kells*. London: Thames and Hudson.
Méniel, P. 1992. *Les sacrifices d'animaux chez les Gaulois*. Paris: Editions Errance.
Méniel, P. 2005. La sépulture humaine et le dépôt d'animaux de Varennes-sur-Seine, Le Marais de Villeroy (Seine-et-Marne). In O. Buchsenschutz, A. Bulard & Th. Lejars (eds), *L'âge du Fer en Île-de-France*, 181–91. Supplement to *Revue archéologique du centre de la France* 26.
Metzner-Nebelsick, C. and Nebelsick, L.D. 1999. Frau und Pferd – ein Topos am Übergang von der Bronze – zur Eisenzeit Europas. *Mitteilungen der Anthropologischen Gesellschaft in Wien* 129, 69–106.
Meyer, K. 1904. The boyish exploits of Finn. *Ériu* 1, 180–90.
Meyer, K. 1911. *Selections from Early Irish Poetry*. London: Constable.
Muhr, K. 2002. The early place-names of County Armagh. *Seanchas Ard Mhacha: Journal of the Armagh Diocesan Historical Society* 19, 1–54.
Muhr, K. 2013. Queen Medb in place-names. In G. Toner and S. Mac Mathúna (eds), *Ulidia 3. Proceedings of the Third International Conference on the Ulster Cycle of Tales, University of Ulster, Coleraine, 22–25 June, 2009*, 49–73. Berlin: curach bhán publications.
Muller, J-C. 1975. La Royauté divine chez les Rukuba (Benue-Plateau State, Nigeria). *L'Homme* 15, 5–27.
Nagy, G. 1992. *Greek Mythology and Poetics*. New York: Cornell University Press.
Nagy, J. F. 1985. *The Wisdom of the Outlaw. The Boyhood Deeds of Finn in Gaelic Narrative Tradition*. Berkeley: University of California Press.
Needham, S. 1991. *Excavations and Salvage at Runnymede Bridge, 1978: the Late Bronze Age Waterfront Site*. London: British Museum Press.
Needham, S. 2000. The development of embossed goldwork in Bronze Age Europe. *Antiquaries Journal* 80, 27–65.
Needham, S. 2000a. Power pulses across a cultural divide: cosmologically driven acquisition between Armorica and Wessex. *Proceedings of the Prehistoric Society* 66, 151–207.

Needham, S., Parfitt, K. and Varndell, G. 2006. *The Ringlemere Cup: precious cups and the beginning of the Channel Bronze Age*. London: British Museum.

Neill, K. 2009. *An Archaeological Survey of County Armagh*. Belfast: Northern Ireland Environment Agency.

Newman, C. 1997. *Tara: an archaeological survey*. Dublin: Royal Irish Academy.

Newman, C. 2007. Procession and symbolism at Tara: analysis of Tech Midchúarta (the 'Banqueting Hall') in the context of the sacral campus. *Oxford Journal of Archaeology* 26, 415–38.

Newman, C. 2009. The sword in the stone: previously unrecognised archaeological evidence of ceremonies of the later Iron Age and early medieval period. In G. Cooney, K. Becker, J. Coles, M. Ryan and S. Sievers (eds), *Relics of Old Decency: archaeological studies in later prehistory. Festschrift for Barry Raftery*, 425–36. Dublin: Wordwell.

Ní Dhonnchadha, M. 2002. Courts and coteries I, 900–1600. In A. Bourke, M. Kilfeather, M. Luddy, M. Mac Curtain, G. Meaney, M. Ní Dhonnchadha, M. O'Dowd and C. Wills (eds), *The Field Day Anthology of Irish Writing, Vol. 4. Irish Women's Writings and Traditions*, 293–303. Cork: Cork University Press.

Ní Dhonnchadha, M. 2002a. Gormlaith and her Sisters, c. 750–1800. In A. Bourke, M. Kilfeather, M. Luddy, M. Mac Curtain, G. Meaney, M. Ní Dhonnchadha, M. O'Dowd and C. Wills (eds), *The Field Day Anthology of Irish Writing, Vol. 4. Irish Women's Writings and Traditions*, 166–249. Cork: Cork University Press.

Nordberg, A. 2009. The grave as a doorway to the Other World. Architectural religious symbolism in Iron Age graves. *Temenos* 45, 35–63.

Nygaard, S. 2016. Sacral rulers in pre-Christian Scandinavia: The possibilities of typological comparisons within the paradigm of cultural evolution. *Temenos* 52, 9–35.

Ó Broin, T. 1974. 'Craebruad': the spurious tradition. *Éigse* 15, 103–13.

Ó Canann, T. G. 2003. Carraig an Dúnáin: probable Ua Canannáin Inauguration Site, *Journal of the Royal Society of Antiquaries of Ireland* 133, 36–67.

Ó Cathasaigh, T. 1983. *Cath Maige Tuired* as an Exemplary Myth. In P. de Brún, S. Ó Coileáin and P. Ó Riain (eds), *Folia Gadelica: Essays presented by former students to R.A. Breathnach*, 1–19. Cork: Cork University Press. Reprinted in M. Boyd (ed.) 2014. *Coire Sois, The Cauldron of Knowledge: a Companion to Early Irish Saga, Tomás Ó Cathasaigh*, 135–54. Notre Dame: University of Notre Dame Press.

Ó Cathasaigh, T. 1984. Pagan survivals: the evidence of early Irish narrative. In P. Ní Chatháin and M. Richter (eds), *Irland und Europa Ireland and Europe. Die Kirche im Frühmittelalter The Early Church*. Stuttgart: Klett-Cotta. Reprinted in M. Boyd (ed.) 2014. *Coire Sois, The Cauldron of Knowledge: a Companion to Early Irish Saga, Tomás Ó Cathasaigh*, 35–50. Notre Dame: University of Notre Dame Press.

Ó Cathasaigh, T. 1996. Gat and *Díberg* in *Togail Bruidne Da Derga*. In A. Ahlqvist, G. W. Banks, R. Latvio, H. Nyberg and T. Sjöblom (eds), *Celtica Helsingiensia. Proceedings from a Symposium on Celtic Studies*. Helsinki: Societas Scientiarum Fennica. Reprinted in M. Boyd (ed.), 2014. *Coire Sois, The Cauldron of Knowledge: a Companion to Early Irish Saga, Tomás Ó Cathasaigh*, 412–21. Notre Dame: University of Notre Dame Press.

Ó Cathasaigh, T. 2010. Kingship in early Irish literature. In *L'Irlanda e gli irlandesi nell'alto medioevo*, 135–51. Spoleto: Fondazione Centro Italiano di Studi sull'Alto Medioevo.

Ó Cathasaigh, T. 2011. Conchobor and his court at Emain. In A. Ahlqvist and P. O'Neill (eds), *Language and Power in the Celtic World. Papers from the Seventh Australian Conference of Celtic Studies, The University of Sydney, 30 September–2 October 2010*, 309–22. Sydney: University of Sydney.

O'Connor, R. 2013. *The Destruction of Da Derga's Hostel. Kingship and Narrative Artistry in a Medieval Irish Saga*. Oxford: Oxford University Press.

O Daly, M. 1960. On the origin of Tara. *Celtica* 5, 186–91.

O Daly, M. 1975. *Cath Maige Mucrama: The battle of Mag Mucrama*. London: Irish Texts Society.

Ó Floinn, R. 2001. Patrons and politics: art, artefact and methodology. In M. Redknap, N. Edwards, S. Youngs, A. Lane and J. Knight (eds), *Pattern and Purpose in Insular Art*, 1–14. Oxford: Oxbow Books.

Ó Floinn, R. 2009. Notes on some Iron Age finds from Ireland. In G. Cooney, K. Becker, J. Coles, M. Ryan and S. Sievers (eds), *Relics of Old Decency: archaeological studies in later prehistory. Festschrift for Barry Raftery*, 199–210. Dublin: Wordwell.

Ó hÓgáin, D. 1987. Magic attributes of the hero in Fenian lore. *Béaloideas* 54–55, 207–42.

Ólafsson, H. 1995. Indo-European horse sacrifice in the *Book of Settlements*. *Temenos* 31, 127–43.

Olivier, L. 1999. The Hochdorf 'princely grave' and the question of the nature of archaeological funerary assemblages. In T. Murray (ed.), *Time and Archaeology*, 109–38. London: Routledge.

Ó Máille, T. 1929. Medb Chruachna. *Zeitschrift für celtische Philologie* 17, 129–46.

O'Meara, J. J. 1951. *The First Version of the Topography of Ireland by Giraldus Cambrensis*. Dundalk: Dundalgan Press.

Ó Néill, P. 1999. The Latin colophon to the *Táin bó Cúailnge* in the Book of Leinster: a critical view of Old Irish literature. *Celtica* 23, 269–75.

O'Rahilly, C. 1967. *Táin Bó Cúalnge from the Book of Leinster*. Dublin: Dublin Institute for Advance Studies.

O'Rahilly, T. F. 1946. *Early Irish History and Mythology*. Dublin: Dublin Institute for Advanced Study.

Ó Ríordáin, B. 1997. A Bronze Age cemetery mound at Grange, Co. Roscommon. *Journal of Irish Archaeology* 8, 43–72.

Ó Ríordáin, B. and Waddell, J. 1993. *The Funerary Bowls and Vases of the Irish Bronze Age*. Galway: Galway University Press.

Ó Súilleabháin, S. 1942. *A Handbook of Irish Folklore*. Dublin: Folklore Society of Ireland.

Palaima, T. G. 1995. The Nature of the Mycenaean *Wanax*: non-Indo-European Origins and Priestly Functions. In P. Rehak (ed.), *The Role of the Ruler in the Prehistoric Aegean*. 119–39. Liège: Université de Liège.

Parfitt, K. 1995. *Iron Age burials from Mill Hill, Deal*. London: British Museum Press.

Parfitt, K. and Green, M. 1987. A chalk figurine from Upper Deal, Kent. *Britannia* 18, 295–8.

Parker Pearson, M. 1999. Food, sex and death: cosmologies in the British Iron Age with particular reference to East Yorkshire. *Cambridge Archaeological Journal* 9, 43–69.

Patay, P. 1990. *Die Bronzegefässe in Ungarn*. Praehistorische Bronzefunde II:10. Munich: C. H. Beck.

Pearce, M. 2013. The Spirit of the Sword and Spear. *Cambridge Archaeological Journal* 23, 55–67.

Petrie, G. 1839. On the history and antiquities of Tara Hill. *Transactions of the Royal Irish Academy* 18, 25–232.

Piggott, S. and Daniel, G. E. 1951. *A Picture Book of Ancient British Art*. Cambridge: Cambridge University Press.

Pollard, J. 2017. The Uffington White Horse geoglyph as sun-horse. *Antiquity* 91, 406–20.

Poux, M. 2003. Clermont-Ferrand (Puy-de-Dôme) Le Brézet. *Gallia* 60, 153–4.

Powell, T. G. E. 1971. From Urartu to Gundestrup: the agency of Thracian metal-work. In J. Boardman, M. A. Brown and T. G. E. Powell (eds), *The European Community in Later Prehistory. Studies in Honour of C.F.C. Hawkes*, 181–210. London: Routledge and Kegan Paul.

Prüssing, G. 1991. *Die Bronzegefässe in Österreich*. Praehistorische Bronzefunde II:5. Stuttgart: Franz Steiner.

Pryor, F. 2001. *Seahenge. New Discoveries in Prehistoric Britain*. London: HarperCollins

Puhvel, J. 1970. Aspects of equine functionality. In J. Puhvel (ed.), *Myth and Law Among the Indo-Europeans. Studies in Indo-European Comparative Mythology*, 159–72. Berkeley: University of California Press.

Quesada-Sanz, F. 1998. From quality to quantity: wealth, status and prestige in the Iberian Iron Age. In D. W. Bailey and S. Mills (eds), *The Archaeology of Value: essays on prestige and the processes of valuation*, 70–96. Oxford: British Archaeological Report S730.

Raftery, B. 1983. *A Catalogue of Irish Iron Age Antiquities*. Marburg: Veröffentlichung des Vorgeschichtlichen Seminars Marburg.

Rees, A. D. and Rees, B. 1961. *Celtic Heritage: ancient tradition in Ireland and Wales*. London: Thames and Hudson.

Richmond, I. A. 1954. Queen Cartimandua. *Journal of Roman Studies* 44, 43–52.

Rodríguez-Corral, J. 2015. Las estatuas-menhir noroccidentales en contexto: conectividad y conexiones materiales durante el Bronce Tardío/Final. *Complutum* 26 (1), 153–72.

Rolley, C. (ed.) 2003. *La tombe princière de Vix*. Paris: Picard.

Russell, M., Cheetham, P., Evans, D., Hambleton, E., Hewitt, I., Manley, H. and Smith, M. 2014. The Durotriges Project, Phase One: an interim statement. *Proceedings of the Dorset Natural History & Archaeological Society* 135, 217–21.

Sarry, F., Courtaud, P. and Cabezuelo, U. 2016. La sépulture multiple laténienne du site de Gondole (Le Cendre, Puy-de-Dôme). *Bulletins et mémoires de la Société d'anthropologie de Paris* 28, 72–83.

Sayers, W. 2012. Netherworld and Otherworld in early Irish literature. *Zeitschrift für celtische Philologie* 59, 201–30.

Scarre, C. 2013. Social Stratification and the State in Prehistoric Europe. In M. Cruz Berrocal, L. García Sanjuán and A. Gilman (eds), *The Prehistory of Iberia. Debating Early Social Stratification and the State*, 382–405. London: Routledge.

Schjødt, J. P. 2010. Ideology of the ruler in pre-Christian Scandinavia: mythic and ritual relations. *Viking and Medieval Scandinavia* 6, 161–94.

Schot, R. 2011. From cult centre to royal centre: monuments, myths and other revelations at Uisneach. In R. Schot, C. Newman and E. Bhreathnach (eds), *Landscapes of Cult and Kingship*, 87–113. Dublin: Four Courts Press.

Schot, R., Newman, C. and Bhreathnach, E. (eds), 2011. *Landscapes of Cult and Kingship*. Dublin: Four Courts Press.

Sergent, B. 1992. L'arbre au pourri. *Études Celtiques* 29, 391–402.

Sharples, N. 2005. Life Histories and the Buildings of the Atlantic Iron Age. In V. Turner, S. Dockrill, R. Nicholson and J. Bond (eds), *Tall Stories: 2 millennia of brochs*, 102–14. Lerwick: Shetland Amenity Trust.

Sheehy, M. 1965. *Pontificia Hibernica: medieval Papal Chancery Documents concerning Ireland 640–1261. Vol. 2.* Dublin: M.H. Gill.

Shepherd, I. A. G. and Shepherd, A. N. 2001. A Cordoned Urn burial with faience from 102 Findhorn, Moray. *Proceedings of the Society of Antiquaries of Scotland* 131, 101–28.

Singor, H. W. 1991. Nine against Troy. *Mnemosyne* 44, 17–62.

Skoglund, P. 2012. Culturally modified trees: a discussion based on rock art images. In A. M. Jones, J. Pollard, M. J. Allen and J. Gardiner (eds), *Image, Memory and Monumentality. Archaeological Engagements with the Material World,* 281–88. Oxford: Prehistoric Society Research Papers 5.

Sørensen, M. L. S. 2004. Stating Identities: the Use of Objects in Rich Bronze Age Graves. In J. Cherry, C. Scarre and S. Shennan (eds), *Explaining Social Change: studies in honour of Colin Renfrew,* 167–76. Cambridge: McDonald Institute for Archaeological Research.

Stead, I. M. 1965. *The La Tène Cultures of Eastern Yorkshire.* York: Yorkshire Philosophical Society.

Stead, I. M. 1991. *Iron Age Cemeteries in East Yorkshire.* London: English Heritage.

Stead, I. and Hughes, K. 1997. *Early Celtic Designs.* London: British Museum Press.

Sterckx, C. 1986. *Eléments de cosmogonie celtique.* Brussels: Éditions de l'Université de Bruxelles.

Sterckx, C. 2009. *Mythologie du monde celte.* Paris: Marabout.

Sterckx, C. 2013. L'enlèvement d'Europe par Zeus: un *rājasūya* grec? *Nouvelle Mythologie Comparée/New Comparative Mythology* 1, 207–15.

Stokes, W. 1893. The voyage of the Húi Corra. *Revue Celtique* 14, 22–69.

Stöllner, T. 2014. Mobility and cultural change of the early Celts: La Tène openwork belt-hooks north and south of the Alps. In P. Barral, J-P. Guillaumet, M-J. Roulière-Lambert, M. Saracino and D. Vitali (eds), *Les Celtes et le Nord de l'Italie (Premier et Second Âges du fer),* 211–30. Dijon: 36e supplément à la *Revue archéologique de l'Est.*

Ström, Å. V. 1959. The King God and his Connection with Sacrifice in Old Norse Religion. In *La regalità sacra. The sacral kingship. Contributions to the central theme of the VIIIth International Congress for the History of Religions (Rome, April 1955)*, 702–15. Leiden: E. J. Brill.

Sundqvist, O. 2012. 'Religious ruler ideology' in pre-Christian Scandinavia. In C. Raudvere and J. P. Schjødt (eds), *More than Mythology. Narratives, ritual practices and regional distribution in pre-Christian Scandinavian religions*, 225–61. Lund: Nordic Academic Press.

Tatár, M. M. 2007. The Myth of Macha in Eastern Europe. *Journal of Indo-European Studies* 35, 323–44.

Tolstoy, N. 2016. *The Mysteries of Stonehenge. Myth and Ritual at the Sacred Centre*. Stroud: Amberley.

Toner, G. 1988. Emain Macha in the literature. *Emania* 4, 32–5.

Toner, G. 2010. Macha and the invention of myth. *Ériu* 60, 81–109.

Tonnochy, A. B. and Hawkes, C. F. C. 1931. The Sacred Tree motive on a Roman bronze from Essex. *Antiquaries Journal* 11, 123–28.

Trachsel, M. 2005. Kriegergräber? Schwertbeigabe und Praktiken ritueller Bannung in Gräbern der frühen Eisenzeit. In R. Karl and J. Leskovar (eds), *Interpretierte Eisenzeiten. Fallstudien, Methoden, Theorie*, 53–82. Linz: Oberösterreichisches Landesmuseum Linz.

Treherne, P. 1995. The warrior's beauty: the masculine body and self-identity in Bronze-Age Europe. *Journal of European Archaeology* 3, 105–44.

Tylor, E. B. 1871. *Primitive Culture: Researches Into the Development of Mythology, Philosophy, Religion, Art and Custom*. London: John Murray.

Uckelmann, M. 2013. *Die Schilde der Bronzezeit in Nord-, West- und Zentraleuropa*. Praehistorische Bronzefunde III:4. Stuttgart: Franz Steiner.

Verger, S. 2013. Partager la viande, distribuer l'hydromel. Consommation collective et pratique du pouvoir dans la tombe de Hochdorf. In S. Krausz, A. Colin, K. Gruel, I. Ralston and T. Dechezleprêtre (eds), *L'âge du fer en Europe. Mélanges offerts à Olivier Buchsenschutz*, 495–504. Bordeaux: Ausonius.

Waddell, J. 1983. Rathcroghan – a Royal site in Connacht. *Journal of Irish Archaeology* 1, 21–46.

Waddell, J. 1988. Excavation at 'Dathi's Mound', Rathcroghan, Co. Roscommon. *Journal of Irish Archaeology* 4, 23–36.

Waddell, J. 2005. *Foundation Myths. The Beginnings of Irish Archaeology*. Bray: Wordwell.

Waddell, J. 2011. Continuity, cult and contest. In R. Schot, C. Newman and E. Bhreathnach (eds), *Landscapes of Cult and Kingship*, 192–212. Dublin: Four Courts Press.

Waddell, J. 2014. *Archaeology and Celtic Myth: an exploration*. Dublin: Four Courts Press.

Waddell, J. 2014a. The Cave of Crúachain and the Otherworld. In J. Borsje, A. Dooley, S. Mac Mathúna and G. Toner (eds), *Celtic Cosmology. Perspectives from Ireland and Scotland*, 77–92. Toronto: Pontifical Institute of Medieval Studies.

Waddell, J. 2017. Equine cults and Celtic goddesses. *Emania* 24, 5–18.

Waddell, J., Fenwick, J. and Barton, K. 2009. *Rathcroghan, Co. Roscommon. Archaeological and Geophysical Survey in a Ritual Landscape*. Dublin: Wordwell.

Warner, R. B. 2006. The Tamlaght hoard and the Creeveroe axe. Two new finds of Late Bronze Age date from near Navan, Co. Armagh. *Emania* 20, 20–8.

Watkins, C. 1979. Is Tre Fír Flathemon: Marginalia to *Audacht Morainn*. *Ériu* 30, 181–98.

Watkins, C. 1981. Language, culture, or history? In C. S. Masek, R. A. Hendrick and M. F. Miller (eds), *Papers from the Parasession on Language and Behavior*, 238–48. Chicago: Chicago Linguistic Society. Reprinted in L. Oliver (ed.), 1994. *Calvert Watkins. Selected Writings, Volume 2*, 663–73. Innsbruck: Institut für Sprachwissenschaft der Universität Innsbruck.

Watkins, C. 1995. *How to Kill a Dragon: aspects of Indo-European poetics*. Oxford: Oxford University Press.

Watson, A. 1981. The king, the poet and the sacred tree. *Études Celtiques* 18, 165–80.

Watson, A. 1986. A structural analysis of *Echtra Nerai*. *Études Celtiques* 23, 129–42.

Williams, R. J., Hart, P. J. and Williams, A. T. L. 1996. *Wavendon Gate. a Late Iron Age and Roman settlement in Milton Keynes*. Aylesbury: Buckingham Archaeological Society.

Wirth, S. 2006. Le mystère de la barque solaire: quelques considérations à propos des décors sur les situles de type Hajdúböszörmény et sur une situle inédite du bronze final. In L. Baray (ed.), *Artisanats, sociétés et civilisations: hommage à Jean-Paul Thevenot*, 331–45. Dijon: Revue Archéologique de l'Est Supplément.

Woodward, A. and Hunter, J. 2015. *Ritual in Early Bronze Age Grave Goods. An Examination of Ritual and Dress Equipment from Chalcolithic and Early Bronze Age Graves in Britain*. Oxford: Oxbow Books.

Wormald, P. 1986. Celtic and Anglo-Saxon kingship: some further thoughts. In P. E. Szarmach (ed.), *Sources of Anglo-Saxon Culture*, 151–83. Kalamazoo: Medieval Institute Publications, Western Michigan University.

Wrigley, C. 1996. *Kingship and State. The Buganda dynasty.* Cambridge: Cambridge University Press.

Wyss, R. 1954. Das Schwert des Korisios zur Entdeckung einer Griechischen Inschrift. *Jahrbuch des Bernischen Historischen Museums in Bern* 34, 201–22.

Wyss, R. 1956. The Sword of Korisios. *Antiquity* 30, 27–8.

Zaroff, R. 2005. Asvamedha – A Vedic horse sacrifice. *Studia Mythologica Slavica* 8, 75–86.